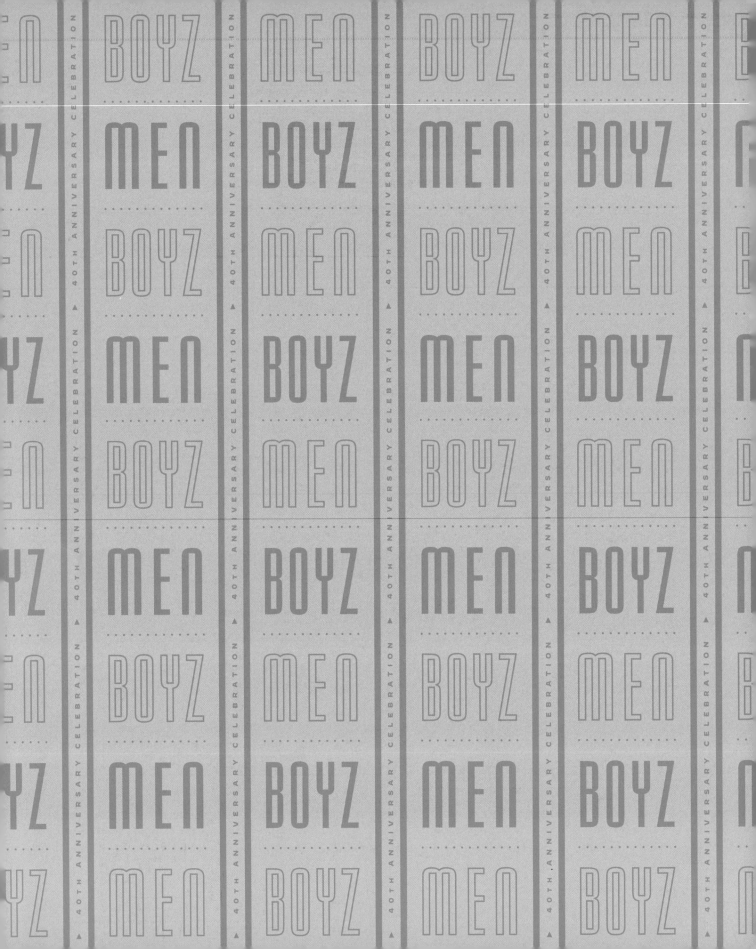

BOYZ II MEN

BOYZ II MEN

NATHAN
40
40
WANYÁ
SHAWN
40
40
MICHAEL

40th
ANNIVERSARY
CELEBRATION

UNAUTHORIZED
&
UNOFFICIAL

JOHN MORRISON
FOREWORD BY ASHLEY OKEN

CONTENTS

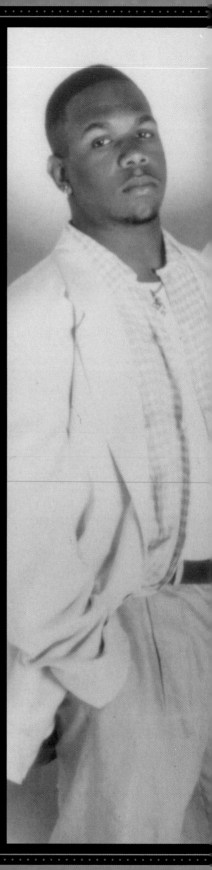

▲ Boyz II Men in 1995.

FOREWORD

When thinking about the origins of my career as a music journalist, I think about my early love of '90s and early 2000s pop music and boy bands. I reminisce about the NSYNC and Backstreet Boys posters that adorned the pink walls of my childhood bedroom and watching the music videos of 98 Degrees and other pop acts with my childhood friends. But the Boyz II Men listening sessions that colored the car rides with my mom throughout Brooklyn and the karaoke nights spent singing "End Of The Road" during tipsy nights in college will forever be core memories.

My love of music always went deeper than the surface level— I was obsessed with knowing the intricacies of the band's origins, the stories behind the hit songs, and how a band's hometown is connected to their music. Any time I hear a Boyz II Men hit track—whether it is "On Bended Knee" or "I'll Make Love To You"—or see a photo of the group from the early 2000s, I am transported back to that time, one of carefree worry, hanging out with my family

after church and taking in music that made us feel understood. As a Black girl growing up in a predominantly white space, Boyz II Men is a group that made me feel seen in a pop music world that did not include a lot of people who looked like me. But the beautiful thing about pop music is its ability to unite people who are different and bond over favorite members, soulfulness and harmonization, interesting facts about discography, and favorite songs.

Trailblazers from the start, Boyz II Men influenced the outfits, harmonies, and choreography of NSYNC, 98 Degrees, and other bands of the bubble gum pop era. 40 years later, the group is still going strong, with tours and residencies abound, their music still having a stronghold on generations of fans.

The *Boyz II Men 40th Anniversary Celebration* encapsulates the Black music tradition that shaped the group and a culture while enthusiastically celebrating these vocalists as the groundbreakers that brought color to universal experiences of love and loss. Drawing on interesting pop culture connections to the group, this homage takes readers through new and riveting bits of context— a jumping-off point that will lead every fan down a rabbit hole of their own and allow readers to see how much adoration there is in this tribute from a hometown fan's perspective.

With the advent of social media, a new breed of pop star, and boy bands receding into the background, it is easy to forget about Boyz II Men and their palace in the broader cultural zeitgeist regarding today's music landscape. Everything needs a starting point, a spark of inspiration that propels so many future pop stars forward. The *Boyz II Men 40th Anniversary Celebration* shows the musical and social importance of these seasoned entertainers and the indelible mark that they have left on pop music.

Far from the end of the road for Boyz II Men, enjoy the journey from the group's humble beginning as gifted teenagers in Philadelphia to their ascent to fame and all the twists and turns in between.

Ashley Oken *is a podcast host, screenwriter, teacher, and entertainment journalist whose work has appeared in MTV News,* New Noise Magazine, ELLE, The New York Times, *and other outlets.*

INTRODUCTION

WITH MORE THAN sixty million albums sold worldwide, multiple Grammy, American Music, *Billboard*, and MTV Awards wins and nominations, and a star on the Hollywood Walk of Fame, few groups have reached heights of mainstream success comparable to Philly R&B legends Boyz II Men. With their soulful songs and complex vocal harmonies rooted in the great Black musical traditions of doo-wop and jazz, the group has been an ambassador for R&B music for the last three decades.

▶ The group poses after winning Favorite Soul/R&B New Artist at the American Music Awards in 1992.

When Shawn Stockman, Wanyá Morris, Michael McCary, and Nathan Morris came together as four ambitious and gifted teenagers from Philadelphia, it is doubtful that they could've predicted where their voices would take them. To date, Boyz II Men have toured in numerous countries on no less than five continents and their catalog contains some of the most beloved songs in the history of popular music.

If you grew up and found or lost love in the 1990s and 2000s, it's likely you have a special relationship with Boyz II Men's music. The group's many hit ballads have grown into enduring staples that have served as the soundtrack to our lives. Since their release, classics like "I'll Make Love To You," "On Bended Knee," "End Of The Road," "A Song For Mama," and "It's So Hard To Say Goodbye to Yesterday" have journeyed with us through the joys and trials of love and loss, marriage and divorce, life and death. Therein lies the true power of Boyz II Men and all great music: Our experiences and touchstone moments will happen whether or not there is musical accompaniment, but these songs beautify and enrich the mundane along with the ecstatic, and they bring color to both the unexpected and the inevitable.

As a Philadelphia native who has lived in the city my entire life, Boyz II Men's music and their story are close to my heart. I have vivid memories of the summer of 1991, eating barbecue at block parties, doing the running man and the Roger Rabbit dances every time "Motownphilly" came blaring through the speakers. My sixth-grade class even sang "End Of The Road" at graduation, the song providing a bittersweet epilogue to our days at Ellwood Elementary in the city's East Oak Lane neighborhood before many of us were bussed up to Woodrow Wilson Middle School in Northeast Philly.

As we come up on forty years of being entertained by these amazing vocalists, it's the perfect time to document and contextualize Boyz II Men's career and their massive influence on pop culture. In the years since their debut, Boyz II Men has weathered lineup changes and the ever-changing landscape of popular music. While they may be many years removed from their heyday at the top of the charts, Boyz II Men remain a vital touring act, traveling the world and performing for adoring fans everywhere.

Whether one considers the group's fresh reimagining of the boy band formula laid down by forebears like The Jackson 5, New Edition, and New Kids On The Block or their role as influencers to the next generation of pop groups like NSYNC, Backstreet Boys, O-Town, and 98 Degrees, Boyz II Men are a link in a long historical chain that unites pop music's past and present. With interviews from musicians that have worked with the group, fans, and journalists alike, we take an in-depth, granular look at the events surrounding the creation of Boyz II Men's music while zooming out to give a bird's-eye view of the music scene and broader cultural zeitgeist that shaped the group's work.

▲ Boyz II Men at Motown Soul
By The Sea II in Montego Bay,
Jamaica, in December 1989.

CHAPTER 1

MOTOWNPHILLY

A Tale of Two Cities and the Art of the Crossover

T O GET A SENSE OF WHERE BOYZ II MEN started and the dizzying commercial heights that they reached, we must first take a look at the soul music legacy of Philadelphia, the record label where they started their career, and its relationship to the concept of "crossing over." "Motownphilly" was not just a simple nod to their hometown and the label that launched them. In many ways, Boyz II Men were the product of two cities, each with their own distinct Black music traditions.

◄ Shawn, Wanyá, Michael, and Nathan perform at Motown Soul By The Sea II in December 1989.

► Berry Gordy
and the Supremes
in 1965.

In the winter of 1959, in Detroit, Michigan, a thirty-year-old veteran of the Korean War named Berry Gordy took an $800 loan from his family and invested it in his dream of founding his own record company. The company that Gordy created, Motown, would go on to have an immeasurable impact on global popular culture. Within a decade of its founding, Motown produced a litany of celebrated acts like the Four Tops, the Supremes, Marvin Gaye and Tami Terrell, the Temptations, Stevie Wonder, Martha & the Vandellas, and more.

For Motown, "crossing over" required the execution of two unlikely feats: a wholesale takeover of Black music and traversing the deep cultural chasm of American racism to capture the ears of white audiences. As an authentic vehicle for Black music expression in the mid- to late twentieth century, R&B—soul music—served as a vessel for the hopes, fears, and aspirations of Black America. Historically, R&B has articulated the deepest desires of Black folks, a dynamic which has often put the music at odds with the cultural palette of a society that sought to marginalize and restrain Black expression as much as possible. Seeing as how R&B is primarily a form in which Black people explore our most intimate thoughts and feelings, it's not exactly the kind of music designed to light up the pop charts. Despite this, there have always been crossover acts, Black musicians whose work appealed to

white audiences and served as a metaphorical bridge. Throughout the 1960s, Motown performed this feat with more success than any of its contemporaries. Concurrent to Motown's rise, the Civil Rights Movement was on its way to winning a handful of important victories and concessions in the struggle to abolish racial apartheid in America.

> *For Motown, "crossing over" required the execution of two unlikely feats: a wholesale takeover of Black music and traversing the deep cultural chasm of American racism to capture the ears of white audiences.*

Throughout his classic 1988 book, *The Death of Rhythm & Blues,* journalist Nelson George eloquently traces the history of twentieth-century Black popular music through its many stylistic evolutions. In the book's sixth chapter, "Crossover: The Death of Rhythm & Blues (1975–1979)," George points to the racial and social dynamics that both led to the invention of R&B and dictated its relationship to the broader American popular culture. George opens the chapter by reminding us that Black American music was born under—and in reaction to—the all-encompassing practice of racial segregation. "Independent record labels, R&B radio, concert venues, retail stores in Black neighborhoods, and the creativity of Black Americans had come together in the thirty years after World War II to create rhythm & blues music," George writes.

With the passage of two important pieces of legislation—the Civil Rights Act of 1964 and the Voting Rights Act of 1965—legal segregation in the US was abolished. This shift in the intent and execution of federal law had sweeping and long-lasting ramifications, and one ancillary result of desegregation was a change in how Black music was marketed to white audiences. George goes on to illustrate that in the decade following Black folks' legal integration into the American mainstream, more space opened for Black music's further assimilation into mainstream American popular culture.

"By the mid-seventies, a segment of Black America had beaten the odds, leaped over the barricade and now lived in parts of the country they would have been lynched in a decade before," George writes. "It struck many of them as time to remove the modifying adjective 'Black' from their lives. It was in this spirit that the term 'crossover' came to dominate all discussion of Black music."

In the summer of 1972, Motown moved its operations from Detroit to Los Angeles. Less than six months after Motown moved to LA, Motown produced the Diana Ross-led Billie Holiday biopic, *Lady Sings the Blues*. This film was followed by *Mahogany* in 1975, *Sparkle* in 1976, and *The Wiz* in 1978. While Detroit may have been Motown's cultural and musical home and literal founding place, it was clear that Berry Gordy had ambitions of taking Hollywood by storm.

In the year prior to Motown's exodus from Detroit, two songwriters—Kenny Gamble and Leon Huff—founded Philadelphia International Records. Their label would in many ways take the baton from Motown and perform the delicate balancing act of serving as the vanguard of Black music while simultaneously crossing over to white audiences. While Philadelphia International's poignant songs and grand orchestral arrangements were distinctive, the sound did not emerge from nowhere. Gable, Huff, and the vocal groups and musicians around them were products of a rich continuum of Philadelphia R&B that preceded them. While Motown and Detroit were carrying Black rhythm & blues into the mainstream, a rich scene populated by skilled vocal groups had sprung up in Philadelphia. Philly soul groups of the 1960s like the Intruders, the Ethics, and the O'Jays were not only the antecedents of the deftly harmonizing doo-wop groups that came before them, they were the immediate forebearers of—and

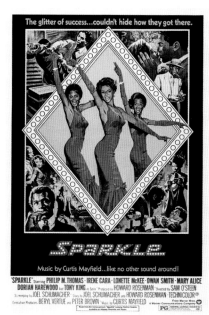

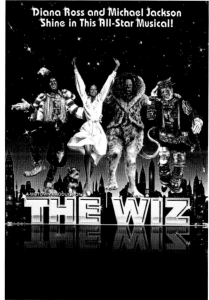

▼ Kenny Gamble
and Leon Huff,
circa 1968.

participants in—the Philly soul revolution that Gamble and Huff spearheaded in the 1970s.

By the end of the 1970s, a new Black cultural movement called hip-hop emerged from the Bronx in New York City, forever changing the conversation around "crossing over." Hip-hop temporarily ruptured the uneasy harmony between Black music, white listeners, and the broader mainstream that had been building since the Civil Rights Movement of the 1960s, ruptures that wouldn't begin to heal until the 1990s.

Boyz II Men's debut single and early successes found the group navigating all this history, as well as the demands of mainstream accessibility. In this way, "Motownphilly" is not just a song, but a work that came in the wake of a long and complicated dance in which the value, respectability, and commercial viability of Black music were constantly being questioned. The group's self-identification as "not too hard/not too soft" is a nod to this dance. Being Black in America is a complicated balancing act in and of itself. Imagine having to do it onstage, under constant spotlight and scrutiny—and with perfect pitch.

When the video for Boyz II Men's debut single, "Motownphilly," premiered in 1991, it was both an introduction and a mission statement. "Motownphilly" positions the group as fresh, youthful updaters of a classic sound. By occasionally cutting to black-and-white scenes of the group dressed in suits, backed by a jazz band, the message is clear: Boyz II Men are a part of a continuum of great twentieth-century Black music that includes R&B, doo-wop, and jazz. As a debut single, "Motownphilly" was—and still is—a stunner. The song's propulsive, up-tempo groove was produced by then-twenty-one-year-old, Atlanta-based wunderkind Dallas Austin. That same year, Austin would score massive hits with TLC's "Ain't 2 Proud 2 Beg" and with "Iesha" and "Playground," both by Another Bad Creation (who were, like Boyz II Men, Michael Bivins signees). Much like his work with TLC and ABC, Austin's production on "Motownphilly" is a mixture of hip-hop-style sampling and R&B-flavored instrumentation. An energetic collage of orchestra hits and synth brass and bass, the song's production was perfectly designed for radio, but the quartet's vocal performance would push it into Walkmans and car stereos nationwide. With the song's contemporary production and the quartet's hip-hop-meets-prep-school fashion sense, we see that Boyz II Men are not retrophiles. This was doo-wop and old-school soul reinterpreted for the hip-hop generation.

It may be hard to imagine today, but in the late 1980s, hip-hop and R&B were at serious odds with one another. Despite sharing common strands of cultural DNA, hip-hop and R&B operated under a set of tensions that divided Black music listeners along both generational and class lines. Though they were the products of the same continuum of Black music that birthed jazz, rock 'n' roll, disco, and more, hip-hop and R&B found themselves conflicting in both aesthetic and mission. Deeply tied to the desires and tastes of older Black Americans in the post-civil rights era, R&B in the 1980s took on a smooth, polished sound that mirrored the assimilationist politics of mainstream, middle-class Black folks. On the other hand, hip-hop music was the new sound of Black American youth, on a trajectory to dominate popular culture by the turn of the century. The loud, aggressive music of acts like Public Enemy and N.W.A was reflective of the triumphs and struggles of Black youth.

> *"Motownphilly" is not just a song, but a work that came in the wake of a long and complicated dance in which the value, respectability, and commercial viability of Black music were constantly being questioned.*

In stark contrast to the slick sound of R&B at the time, hip-hop in the 1980s was as uncompromising thematically as it was sonically. With both genres struggling for the hearts and minds of Black America, the schism between hip-hop and R&B played itself out on Black radio. Many of the old guard gatekeepers of commercial Black radio were resistant to rap music early on. Despite its popularity, program directors and jocks still preferred the sound of R&B to rap. With many commercial Black stations like Power 99/WUSL in Philadelphia and WPGC-FM in DC promoting "no rap weekdays" and effectively relegating hip-hop to late-night/weekend mix shows, it was clear that older Black gatekeepers still held the power to reflect their preferences in the station's programming.

> *With both genres struggling for the hearts and minds of Black America, the schism between hip-hop and R&B played itself out on Black radio.*

Young hip-hop fans naturally bucked against rap's marginalization on Black radio but held little institutional power to change it. In a *Washington Post* piece from 1991, a seventeen-year-old rap fan named N'Dieye Gray complained that Black radio's hostility to rap was "indicative of teenagers not having a voice in what's played." Representing the youthful, confrontational energy of Gen X, hip-hop in the 1980s not only challenged the musical rules; its brash and sometimes playful vulgarity flew in the face of established societal norms. On the other hand, R&B had smoothed out most of its rough edges by the 1980s. The slick, lush sounds of Anita Baker, Freddie Jackson, and Peabo Bryson became the soundtrack of the aspirations of upwardly mobile Black baby boomers across the country. While this gulf between hip-hop and R&B was very real, a few flashes of cohesion sprung up in the form of Teddy Riley's new jack swing, the music of New Edition, and London-based soundsystem-turned-R&B act, Soul II Soul. No one could have predicted that by 1991, a quartet of performing-arts-schooled youngsters from Philadelphia would arrive with a fresh new sound that would go a long way towards striking harmony between the two prevailing forms of Black musical expression.

Colorful, upbeat, and fun, the "Motownphilly" video and the song's lyrics presented Boyz II Men as a clean-cut alternative to the hardcore hip-hop acts that dominated the early 1990s—whether the contrast was intentional or not. As the quartet sang and danced before notable Philadelphia landmarks, viewers also get a sense of the place the band came from. The video deftly cuts between choreographed dances at the Penn's Landing waterfront along the Delaware River

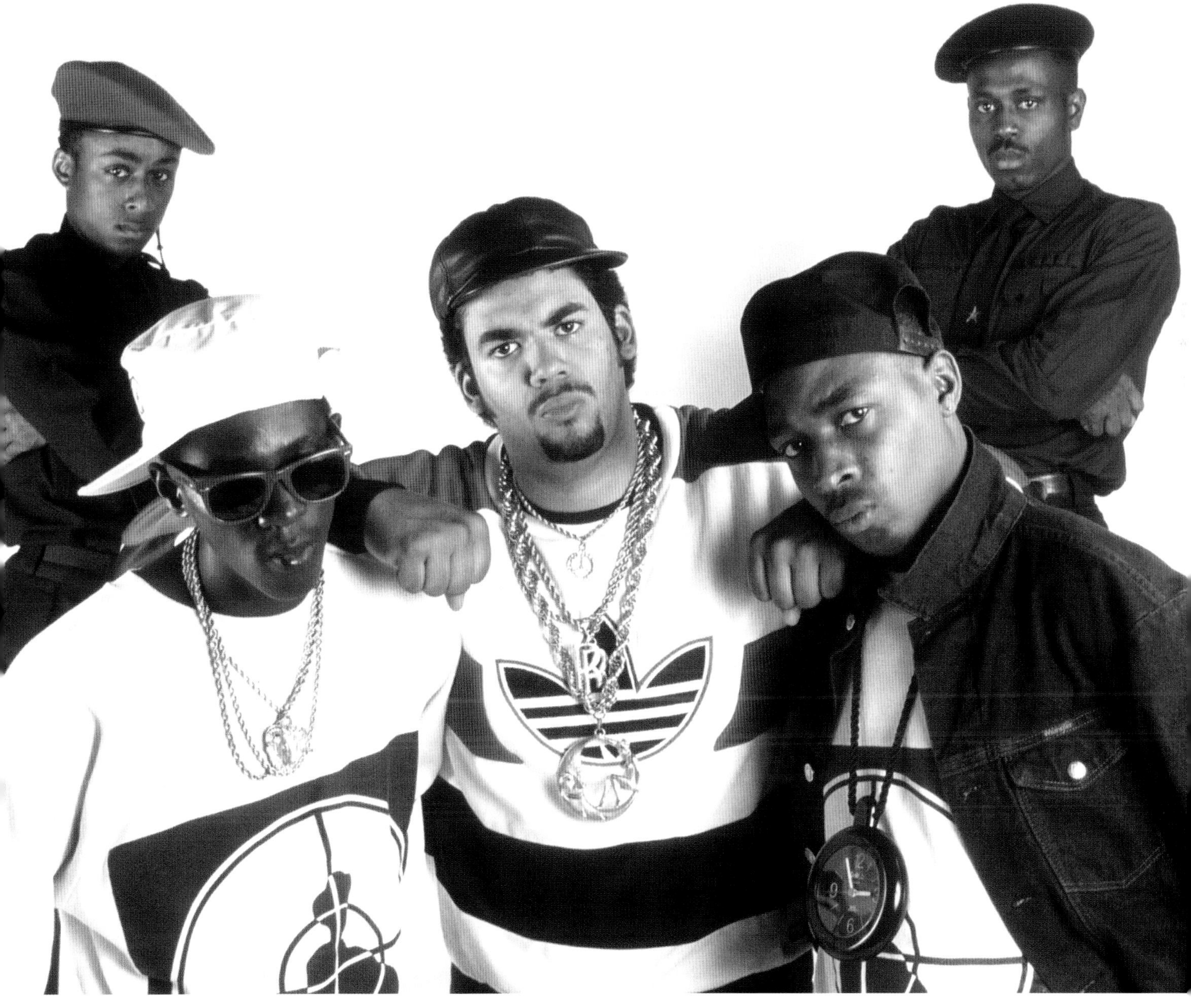

▼ Public Enemy in 1988.

▲ Boyz II Men with
Flavor Flav of Public
Enemy in 1992.

to Geno's Steaks on 9th Street near the Italian Market. Nate and Shawn were shown chilling across the street from the Dickens Inn before the group cruised down the storied South Street strip in a drop-top Mercedes Benz on a bright, sunny day.

While the video's depiction of Philadelphia was that of a bustling metropolis full of fun and music, the underlying reality was that in the early 1990s, Philadelphia was plagued by poverty and violence. The story of Boyz II Men as a group begins at the Philadelphia High School for Creative and Performing Arts (CAPA), but each of the group members grew up in separate neighborhoods and under varying personal circumstances. Nate Morris grew up in South Philly, Shawn Stockman in Southwest Philly, Mike McCary in Logan, and Wanyá Morris in North Philly. CAPA may have provided a refuge in which the Boyz could express themselves creatively, but nothing could've shielded four Black teenagers from the realities of life and crime in Philadelphia in the 1980s. Speaking on the harsh environment he grew up in, Michael McCary explained, "Logan's one of the biggest crime areas in Philly. It was kind of hard coming out every day and going to different parts of the city to sing while all your friends are slinging dope and doing all the things you were trying to stay away from."

Still reeling from the impact of the crack cocaine epidemic, a notorious opiate trade, and generational poverty, Philadelphia saw a then-record 497 homicides in the year prior to the release of "Motownphilly." Obviously, none of this is addressed in the song or the video, but this specter of violence and misery makes the joy expressed in "Motownphilly" all the more dramatic and rewarding. Thematically, the song both celebrates the city of Philadelphia and details the first steps the group would take to transcend it. In an incredibly slick and savvy move, the band baked its own origin story in the song's lyrics.

> *["Motownphilly"] both celebrates the city of Philadelphia and details the first steps the group would take to transcend it.*

But before the success of "Motownphilly," Boyz II Men were just five guys with talent and an ambitious streak, which led them into a very lucky meeting. On May 10, 1989, Michael, Nate, Shawn, Wanyá, and Marc Nelson, a Boyz II Men founding member and future member of Az Yet, finessed their way into Powerhouse, an annual concert hosted by Philly radio juggernaut WUSL Power 99 at the old Civic Center building on 34th Street. With R&B royalty like Natalie Cole, Keith Sweat,

▼ Bell Biv DaVoe in the studio in 1989. (Michael Bivins is in the center.)

Cherelle, and Patti LaBelle present, the boys were in their element. The quintet's initial plan was to meet and audition for Will Smith backstage. Instead, the group ended up linking with Michael Bivins of New Edition and the then-newly formed trio of Bell Biv DeVoe, which featured Bivins along with New Edition members Ricky Bell and Ronnie DeVoe.

Bivins' memorable fifth-verse rap on "Motownphilly" summarizes that fateful day in Philly when he met the group and they first sang for him. He takes a bit of creative license in his verse by excluding Nelson (remember, there were five guys present at that audition, not four). Also, the group did not sing the doo-wop-style harmony break that we hear on the record. The group actually sang an a cappella version of New Edition's titanic ballad "Can You Stand The Rain" during that fated meeting.

This song choice was not the only nod to New Edition. The group's name was taken from the song "Boys To Men," the closer from New Edition's 1988 album, *Heart Break*. As the most prominent Black male vocal group of the 1980s, New Edition were a north star of sorts for Boyz II Men. This admiration combined with Bivins' aspirations to move into managing and developing groups was a match made in heaven. Two weeks after exchanging numbers at Powerhouse, Nate Morris called Bivins every day for a month, talking about all things Boyz II Men-related. Eventually Morris asked Bivins if he'd consider managing the group. This relationship with Bivins would be the key factor in ushering the group into the record industry and their eventual deal with Motown. But when "Motownphilly" hit the streets in 1991, one would be hard-pressed to predict that these four guys from Philly were poised to dominate the 1990s.

U KNOW

"[Boyz II Men] attracted good people and that says something about the quality of their art and the quality of who they were." —Daria Marmaluk-Hajioannou, musician and former Stonecreek studio manager

► The Boyz,
circa 1988.

LIVE FROM THE 215: PHILLY'S MUSICAL GIANTS

Philadelphia is a music city, producing a long list of hitmakers through the decades. Here are some icons of yesterday and today that any Philly music fan should know.

▶ KENNY GAMBLE & LEON HUFF

The songwriting and production duo of Kenny Gamble and Leon Huff have had an incalculable influence on music, both in Philadelphia and around the world. Founded in 1971, Gamble & Huff's label, Philadelphia International Records, produced some of the best soul music of the era. The music that Gamble, Huff, and PIR made during this time was characterized by sweeping orchestral arrangements and beautifully written songs about love, loss, community, and politics. Classics like the O'Jays' "I Love Music," Harold Melvin & The Blue Notes' "Wakeup Everybody," and McFadden & Whitehead's "Ain't No Stoppin' Us Now" are timeless classics reflective of the special magic that Gamble & Huff's partnership could conjure.

▶ MFSB

MFSB (aka Mother, Father, Sister, Brother) was the house band that played on countless Gamble, Huff, and Philadelphia International classics. Formed around the rhythm section of drummer Earl Young, guitarist Norman Harris, and bassist Ronnie Baker, MFSB's stacked lineup of gifted musicians were integral to PIR's impressive run of hit records in the 1970s. From Harold Melvin & The Bluenotes' "The Love I Lost" to Lou Rawls' "You'll Never Find Another Love Like Mine," MFSB's catalog has ensured that they'll be remembered alongside Motown's Funk Brothers and Capitol Records' Wrecking Crew as one of the greatest house bands in the history of recorded music.

▶ PATTI LABELLE

A fierce and bombastic singer, Patti LaBelle is one of the few artists whose dominance stretches across multiple decades. For the first part of her career, Patti LaBelle sang with the Bluebelles, one of the finest female vocal groups in Philly in the 1960s. By the 1970s, she formed LaBelle with Nona Hendryx and raced to the top of the charts with the indelible hit "Lady Marmalade." In addition to her work with groups, Patti LaBelle is one of the greatest solo vocalists to come out of the city of Philadelphia. Her 1980s hits, like "If Only You Knew," are some of the most enduring of the decade.

LADY B

In many ways, Philly rapper and radio personality Wendy Clark, aka Lady B, was the city's first hip-hop star. The West Philly native was discovered while working at the Kim Graves nightclub in downtown Philadelphia, where she'd often get on the mic and rap. In 1979, Lady B released "To The Beat Y'all," a bouncy, disco-flavored tune that earned her recognition as the first woman to release a solo rap single by the Guinness Book of World Records. In addition to her contributions in the studio and onstage, Lady B was the host of Street Beat, one of the first all-rap radio shows in the world.

SCHOOLLY D

To refer to Jesse Weaver Jr., aka Schoolly D, as a hip-hop pioneer would be an understatement. As one of the first Philly rappers of the 1980s to break out of the region and make an impression nationally, Schoolly's impact has been felt globally. His single "P.S.K. (What Does It Mean?)" has been sampled on countless hip-hop, R&B, pop, and rock songs by everyone from Eminem and Notorious B.I.G. to Mary J. Blige and Siouxsie & the Banshees. Schoolly's 1986 "Saturday Night" is considered the first gangsta rap song, influencing West Coast legends like Ice-T and N.W.A.

DJ JAZZY JEFF & THE FRESH PRINCE

After solidifying themselves as Philly rap legends, DJ Jazzy Jeff & the Fresh Prince went on to become one of the first true crossover acts in rap. Blessed with the rare ability to temper virtuosity with accessibility, the group backed their catchy, family-friendly songs with Will's dizzying wordplay and Jeff's lightning-quick turntable scratching. This formula made Jeff and Will stars, and songs like "Parents Just Don't Understand," "Brand New Funk," and "Summertime" are global classics.

CHRISTIAN MCBRIDE

Bassist, bandleader, and composer Christian McBride is one of the finest musicians in contemporary jazz. A CAPA alum who attended the school at the same time as Boyz II Men, McBride has played with a number of jazz legends including Benny Golson, Wynton Marsalis and Freddie Hubbard, McCoy Tyner, George Duke, and more. A skilled and versatile player, McBride's current band, Christian McBride's New Jawn, tackles a variety of styles ranging from free improvisation to bebop.

THE ROOTS

In 1987, CAPA students Tariq Trotter and Ahmir Thompson formed a musical partnership that would change the course of Philadelphia's music scene and hip-hop at large. In the thirty-eight years since, the Roots have revolutionized hip-hop's approach to live performance and built one of the greatest catalogs in rap music. By incorporating live instrumentation into their sound, the Roots have influenced generations of musicians and opened the possibilities of how musicians can play hip-hop. Albums like Do You Want More?!!!??!, Illadelph Halflife, and Things Fall Apart are certified classics that have changed the sound of Hip-Hop music.

JAZMINE SULLIVAN

A Philly native and CAPA alum, Jazmine Sullivan is one of the most celebrated voices in contemporary R&B. Blessed with prodigious vocal talent at a young age, Sullivan got her start as a teenager, singing at Philly's legendary open mic night, the Black Lily, backed by the Roots and hosted every Tuesday night at the Five Spot in Philly's Old City section. Once Sullivan made her debut in 2008 with the album Fearless, she was without question one of the most exciting acts in Black music. Since then, albums like 2010's Love Me Back, 2015's Reality Show, and 2021's Heaux Tales have been hailed as beloved contemporary R&B classics.

CHAPTER 2

A UNIQUE ATTRACTION

COMING TOGETHER AT CAPA

BOYZ II MEN, AS THE WORLD CAME TO know them, started in 1989, but the group's origins go back a little further, to a group called Unique Attraction. Formed in 1985 at the School for Creative and Performing Arts in South Philly, Unique Attraction was both the precursor to Boyz II Men and their original incarnation. The story goes that one day, Nathan was singing in class when his teacher ordered him to stop. Instead of stopping, Nathan sang even louder and was joined by his classmate, Marc Nelson. Their teacher kicked both boys out of class and they became fast friends, bonding over a shared love of New Edition.

◄ Boyz II Men performing in 1988.

▼   The CAPA Choir performs in 2016, carrying on the school's long tradition of artistic and creative expression.

Nathan and Marc then recruited George Baldi, Jon Shoats, and Marguerite Walker into the group. In 1987, freshman Wanyá Morris joined the group, but in 1988, Walker, Baldi, and Shoats graduated and left CAPA. School choir member Shawn Stockman joined the group next, with Michael McCary then joining as the fifth and final piece.

In the fall of 1977, a Philadelphia teacher and administrator named John R. Vannoni had a vision for a new school and a unique educational opportunity for high schoolers in the city. A lover of jazz and classical music and English and American literature, Vannoni's life revolved around both education and the arts. Vannoni was also a Philadelphia native who graduated from South Philadelphia High School in 1944, before enrolling in the Navy less than a year before the end of World War II. When the former aircraft gunner returned home from the war, he earned his bachelor's in education from West Chester University before earning a master's degree in English from Temple University. While working as the head of the English department at Benjamin Franklin High, Vannoni was selected by the Board of Education to be the first principal of the Philadelphia School for Creative and Performing Arts (aka CAPA).

In sharp contrast to other Philadelphia district schools, CAPA was billed as "the district's first effort at voluntary desegregation" by a *Philadelphia Daily News* article in December 1977. Like many northern cities, Philadelphia and its school system still struggled under a form of de facto segregation over two decades after the Supreme Court's landmark *Brown v. the Board of Education* ruling outlawed the practice in schools. In the years following the federal ruling mandating the desegregation of schools, education in the United States remained an apartheid institution. In Philadelphia, famous grassroots struggles to integrate schools like Girard College in North Philly raged on throughout the 1950s and much of the 1960s. Mandatory busing was the predominant method of desegregating schools in the city. Often initiated by court order or school board mandate, mandatory busing sought to diversify the racial makeup of schools by sending students to schools outside their communities.

CAPA was different. The school allowed parents and students from around the city to apply freely regardless of their racial background or location. CAPA would be the first Philadelphia school to openly enroll students of all races and structure their educational experience around the arts. CAPA was set to enroll 300 students from around the area and open on February 1, 1978. Vannoni had only been appointed as the school's founding principal on December 19, 1977, meaning he had roughly two months to assemble a staff and build a curriculum for the school. He cherry-picked a cadre of talented teachers he'd worked with in the past and immediately set about the task of creating the new school.

> *CAPA would be the first Philadelphia school to openly enroll students of all races and structure their educational experience around the arts.*

Originally located at Broad and Spruce Streets, those early days of CAPA found Vannoni and his staff flying by the seat of their pants. With classes concentrated into various artistic disciplines, students interested in music, drama, sculpture, dance, painting, and more were encouraged to apply and receive an arts-centered education unlike any in the city. The school also offered creative writing courses and a standard academic program. The classes were often divided by chalkboards instead of proper walls, but the dedicated staff and the ambitious vision that birthed the school ensured its eventual success. Vannoni opted to hire teachers who were passionate about the arts, bypassing the typical method of hiring teachers with seniority, which brought objections from the Philadelphia Federation of Teachers union. But in a *Philadelphia Daily News* piece from January 1978, Vannoni's priorities are laid out clearly: "Vannoni wants an entire staff with a heightened sensitivity to the arts. He wants English teachers who can supplement the creative writing courses, math teachers who dabble in photography. 'Someone who wants to transfer here because it's a convenient Center City location—that does nothing for our program,' he said."

With this kind of careful and thoughtful intention as part of its founding, it's no surprise that the Philadelphia High School of Creative and Performing Arts has grown into one of the cornerstones of Philadelphia public education and the city's music scene. In the forty-seven years since it was founded, CAPA has nurtured several gifted and notable artists, including Jazmine Sullivan, the actor/singer Leslie Odom Jr., jazz giants Christian McBride and Joey DeFrancesco, and Boyz II Men classmates Tariq "Black Thought" Trotter and Ahmir "Questlove" Thompson of legendary Philly hip-hop band the Roots.

By the time Nate, Wanyá, Shawn, and Michael got to CAPA, the school's hallways and classrooms were rich with music and art. In his 2013 book, *Mo' Meta Blues: The World According to Questlove*, Thompson described the wildly diverse and creative scene at CAPA in the 1980s. "The first few days at CAPA redefined 'culture shock' for me," he wrote. "I went

▲ Questlove performs during the 2024
Roots Picnic at The Mann in Philadelphia.

from a small school of twenty to a school of two thousand, and the first day alone was surreal. It's like I had been transported into the movie *Fame*. Look, there's a knot of goth kids. There are some ballerinas over there in the corner. There are jazz students with their instruments out in the lunchroom."

CAPA proved to be a perfect situation for Nathan, Shawn, Michael, and Wanyá. With Michael hailing from Logan, Wanyá coming from North Philly, Nate from South Philly, and Shawn from Southwest Philly, CAPA—and its open enrollment policy—was the variable that would ultimately bring them together. Each of the four core members were gifted singers who used music as a means of escaping the harsh realities of life in their neighborhoods. Shawn was the product of a large family. His parents, JoAnn Stockman and Thurman Sanders, raised ten children in their household, eight boys and two girls. Naturally, money was tight, but Shawn has spoken fondly of his childhood and the joy that music brought him. In an interview for *Us II You*, the group's 1995 memoir, Shawn recalled his mother's musical tastes as an important inspiration in his childhood. "My mother listened to old Teddy Pendergrass albums, LTD, Ohio Players, Michael Jackson, and Stevie Wonder," he said. "She loved Barry White and loves him to this day."

Wanyá came from a much smaller family, with just one brother and two sisters, but initially found a large extended family in the form of his neighbors in North Philly's Richard Allen Projects. "We are all from urban neighborhoods in Philly," he said in *Us II You*. "These were loving communities that turned a corner during our lifetimes. As we grew up, the neighborhoods grew worse. Bad things happened all around us. Gangs and drugs were on the rise. Drugs were available, drugs were as available as a pack of cigarettes. I sat there and I watched a lot of things happen."

CAPA not only offered the boys an opportunity to develop their craft through practice, but it also helped open their musical palettes, exposing them to a variety of music.

Like his bandmates, Michael grew up in a rough neighborhood and gravitated to music at a young age. He had two brothers and a sister, and his family were key influences on his musical tastes, playing records and the radio constantly in the house. Michael enjoyed classic vocal groups like the Temptations and contemporary groups like New Edition equally. Meanwhile, Nathan was the youngest of Gail Harris and Alphonso Morris Sr.'s four children. Growing up in South Philly, Nathan's family struggled to make ends meet, sometimes going without basic utilities like electricity, water, and gas. But Nathan was naturally musical and a gifted singer and trumpet player, the perfect candidate to audition and enroll at CAPA.

CAPA not only offered the boys an opportunity to develop their craft through practice, but it also helped open their musical palettes, exposing them to a variety of music that they were previously unfamiliar with. In a 2006 interview with *Black Voice News*, Shawn explained how those CAPA years affected the group, saying, "We would not have met if we hadn't attended CAPA. In the neighborhoods we came from, it was not customary to listen to Bach or Beethoven."

A key part of the young men's musical evolution during this time was their choir teacher, David J. King. In addition to his work at CAPA, King was a member of the American Guild of Organists and his musical prowess was unmatched. In the *Black Voice News* interview, Shawn remembered King as firm but essential to Boyz II Men's growth. "Mr. David King taught us everything we know," he said. "He was tough on us, but we know now that it was for a reason."

The boys' four years at the school provided them with an environment ripe with both music and mischief. Between singing in choir and studying the work of musical greats ranging from Beethoven to James Brown, the boys pulled pranks like mooning people in the hallway and handcuffing unfortunate freshmen in the bathroom. The group also practiced intensely—and fought like brothers.

In the group's documentary *Then II Now*, Shawn talked about those early years and the growing pains that came along with them. "It's because we were group members before we were actual friends," he said. "At first, we argued every day. If it wasn't about little trivial things and girls and all this other stuff, it was about something else. During the course of everything, we became closer and now we're the best of friends."

> *"During the course of everything, we became closer and now we're the best of friends."*

The camaraderie built during these years undoubtedly prepared the group for their future as Boyz II Men. But before they adopted that now-famous moniker, the group had to find its legs under another name: Unique Attraction.

"Unique Attraction—ugh, so gross!" said Shawn in a 2021 interview with *People*, poking

◄ Boyz II Men circa 1990.

▶ Philadelphia has a long history of the fight for equality.

▶ The Trammps
in 1977.

42

fun at Boyz II Men's original name. "It was such a Philadelphia name. If you grew up in Philadelphia, you know exactly what I'm talking about. It was cheesy, but it was the vibe back then."

Despite Shawn's present feelings about the name, Unique Attraction was an important stepping-stone in the group's early history. Whether intentionally or not, Unique Attraction and their very "Philadelphia name" were the latest link in a continuum of Philly rhythm & blues vocal groups that stretched back to at least the mid-twentieth century. When doo-wop began to take shape as a genre in the 1940s, Black America was in the midst of the mass exodus from the American South now known as the Great Migration.

In the immediate aftermath of slavery's abolition, life as a free man, woman, or child in the South was no less harsh and arbitrarily cruel for Black folks. While Black workers were no longer confined to the plantation by law, they often found themselves economically coerced into performing the same tasks, on the same land, for the same men they had once called master. Militia-style formations of white men were deputized throughout the South and tasked with enforcing the law, which often meant harassing and arresting Black people for irrational, minor offenses such as assembling after dark or legal vagaries like "idleness." At the same time, lynching

reached its height in the decades immediately following abolition.

It was against this social and political backdrop that the blues formed in the South. These events also initiated the movement of an estimated six million African Americans throughout the country over the next six decades. Black American music culture took root and evolved wherever its practitioners went. The promise of jobs in the industrial sector drew African Americans to urban centers like Chicago, Detroit, New York, and Philadelphia. The cultural fabric of the blues remained with the people who sang it, and the Great Migration spread the music nationwide. The popular Black vocal rhythm & blues that emerged in American cities in the 1940s and 1950s would be called "doo-wop" years after its commercial height and eventual decline.

Doo-wop was a combination of the blues, jazz, and Black church music. A decidedly urban music, doo-wop was the sound of Black Southerners wrestling with the trials of love and loss in the big city. In doo-wop, the lead voice and the accompanying voices around it sounded almost like jazz, in which the lead instrumentalist would take a solo, and the band around them would support the soloist rhythmically and harmonically. Most doo-wop songs were based on the I–V–vi–IV, a chord progression built using the first, fifth, sixth, and fourth chords of a musical scale. Combine the doo-wop chord progression with four- or five-part vocal harmonies and you get a sound that pulled from a variety of other genres but maintained a formula that made it distinct. The genre reached its height in the 1950s and has arguably influenced every form of popular vocal music that followed.

In Philadelphia, the doo-wop sound and the vocal groups that sang it were particularly strong. Throughout the 1950s, Philly groups like the Silhouettes ("Get a Job" 1957), Lee Andrews and the Hearts—a doo-wop quintet fronted by Questlove's father, Lee Andrews—and the Turbans ("When You Dance" 1955) released smash hits that transcended the confines of the region and became major hits nationwide. By the 1960s, the doo-wop craze had all but died, but the spirit of that great vocal tradition lived on in many of the new vocal groups that formed on street corners, in playgrounds, and in clubs throughout the city.

In an interview with *Spin*, singer and drummer Earl Young of the Trammps and MFSB remembered the club scene in the 1960s as a hotbed for local vocal groups. "Scotty's on 52nd [Street]. I think it was 52nd and Locust," he said. "We did a lot of the gigs at the Cadillac Club. A lot of these clubs ain't around anymore. They've been gone. We did the Highline, it's called the Stinger now [the Stinger Club is located above the legendary Sid Booker's take-out shrimp and seafood spot]."

Sixties vocal groups like the O'Jays, the Ethics, and the Blue Notes were not only precursors to the storied Philadelphia International Records sound that would follow in the 1970s, many of their members would end up cutting hit records for the Gamble and Huff stable. As a vocal group, Boyz II Men are a part of this Philly soul music tradition, taking direct inspiration from the music that came before them. In a 2010 interview with

U KNOW

"Much of what the world knows and loves about the sound of Boyz II Men—the influence of Take 6, the bespoke production of Babyface, and the early mentorship of Michael Bivins aside—is a direct byproduct of the vocal program at the Philadelphia High School for Creative and Performing Arts. The group have been steadfast ambassadors of the harmonic excellence and staggering talent that the school has become known for churning out."
—*Karas Lamb, music journalist and CAPA alum*

the *Gainesville Sun*, Shawn acknowledged this tradition as a formative influence on the band's work: "We were fortunate to have that type of music and that type of history at our disposal while we were growing up. If that music wasn't on the radio, then our parents were playing it at home. You couldn't help but be influenced by that sound and by Gamble and Huff. It was just something that was in our blood."

In many ways, Unique Attraction was modeled after the classic Philly vocal groups that placed importance on precise vocal harmonies that could only be produced by tireless practice and intimate communication between singers. In an interview for *Us II You*, Nate recalled one of the bathroom singing sessions that led Unique Attraction to find the crucial component to the group's sound: the bass.

"We were sort of organizing a singing group, using different members of the choir," he remembered. "Finally we had Shawn, Wanyá, a friend named Marc Nelson, and myself together, singing as a group. We hadn't met Michael yet. One day, the four of us were in the bathroom, practicing in there. The song was "Can You Stand The Rain?" by New Edition. Michael happened to come in and without anyone saying a word, he started singing, adding the bass note. It was what we needed, tied the whole together."

With the introduction of Michael's bass,

Unique Attraction had a complete sound, but they still weren't completely comfortable with their name. New Edition's 1988 album, *Heart Break*, had given them a signature song to showcase their talents with "Can You Stand The Rain?" but it would be another song from the album that would provide a proper name for the burgeoning group. "Boys To Men" is *Heart Break*'s closing salvo. Much like "Motownphilly" would serve as a future mission statement for Nate, Michael, Shawn, and Wanyá at the beginning of their careers, "Boys To Men" served a similar purpose for New Edition at the height of theirs. A dreamy ballad with Johnny Gill's powerful lead taking center stage, the song's lyrics speak to the group's desire to grow up and take command of their careers and lives as men. The growing pains that inevitably come along with childhood stardom have never been easy to navigate. The annals of history and the pages of tabloids worldwide are filled with the tragic stories of gifted youngsters who just could not survive fame and public scrutiny with their health and sanity intact. New Edition famously struggled with this dynamic, and "Boys To Men" is a plea for perseverance as much as it is an ode to maturation.

Replacing the word "to" with the double I Roman numeral, Boyz II Men was born. Nate, Michael, Shawn, Wanyá, and Marc then set about making a name for themselves as a

▼ A view of the Uptown
Theater in Philadelphia in
May 1963.

quintet. According to Shawn, the first time Boyz II Men performed in public was in 1988 at the Impulse Club (formerly the Cadillac Club) in North Philly. By all accounts, the performance went well, and the boys blew the unsuspecting crowd away with their vocal skills. In an interview for the 1995 book *Us II You*, Shawn tells the story of that first performance at Impulse.

"We sang three songs," Shawn recalled. "'Can You Stand The Rain?,' 'A Thousand Miles Away,' and 'What's Your Name?' The reaction was whooah. Something good was going on. We had tough times when we were starting out. We weren't best friends yet. We had to work on respecting each other, understanding where each one came from. But from the start we had this common ground: the music. The more we sang together, the more we blended."

During this time, Boyz II Men also cut their teeth playing talent shows at NU-TEC (formerly the legendary Uptown Theater in North Philly) and CAPA. Being a performing arts school jam-packed with gifted young people eager to show off their skills, CAPA's talent shows were not just fun, they were serious competition. In a 2014 *Huffington Post* interview, Black Thought recalled when the Roots faced off against Boyz II Men at one of CAPA's notoriously competitive talent shows.

"The talent shows were, like, huge, man," Black Thought related. "The production was an annual thing. They would call it Sentimental Journey. So, you know, it was all about who was performing at Sentimental Journey this year. Our rivals wound up being Boyz II Men."

"They used to cheat with glitter," Questlove added in the article. "Girls would start swooning. They would have glitter and the top hats."

"You couldn't help but be influenced by that sound and by Gamble and Huff. It was just something that was in our blood."

While honing their presentation and vocal skills, Boyz II Men began plotting a way to get a foot into the proverbial door of the record industry. While Philadelphia has always been rich with talent, no major music industry infrastructure exists here. None of the major labels or talent agencies have offices in Philly, and in the pre-internet 1980s and early 1990s, this lack of industry institutions was a serious hindrance to the growth of local acts. Many talented locals found themselves hitting a glass ceiling in Philly, and many opted to move to more prominent industry centers like New York or Los Angeles. But Boyz II Men didn't do that. Instead of going to the places where the record industry existed, they simply waited for the industry to come to them.

FAMOUS CAPA CLASSMATES

WHILE BOYZ II MEN ARE AMONG THE MOST FAMOUS CAPA ALUMNI, THEY ARE NOT THE SCHOOL'S ONLY CLAIMS TO FAME.

While the members of Boyz II Men formed what would be Philly's most famous R&B band, two of their classmates were in the process of building the city's most beloved hip-hop band. Before the Roots went on to release over a dozen albums, tour the world, and reintroduce the live band to hip-hop, the group's founders, Tariq "Black Thought" Trotter and Ahmir "Questlove" Thompson, were CAPA students.

Drawn together by a shared love of hip-hop and nurtured by the creatively fertile environment at CAPA, Trotter and Thompson spent those early days forming a bond through the most elemental forms of musical expression: the human voice and the drum. Trotter was a prodigious improviser who gave the band street credibility that remains nearly forty years after their founding. In a 2017 interview with the *Philadelphia Metro*, Trotter reflected on his time at CAPA and how he and Thompson had very different experiences in their teen years. "I was so much in the streets at the time. . . . I was exposed to a more street side of the city and running free before school, during school hours, and after school. Ahmir was more sheltered and more laser-focused on becoming a professional musician."

A seasoned drummer and musical director in his father's doo-wop and soul band by the time he was in high school, Thompson brought stage-readiness and experience to the group. In his book *Mo' Meta Blues*, Thompson explained that being a hip-hop head, he found himself caught in the middle of an intense ideological and aesthetic war between the students of CAPA's jazz department. "Other high schools are dominated by jocks . . . CAPA was dominated by jazz kids. . . . The two groups [traditionalists and outsiders] were Bloods and Crips, in a way, but they were united by a common hatred for hip-hop. So here I came, wading into the middle of that divide."

After cycling through a few name changes—including Black to The Future and Radioactivity—the Roots were born. Despite Trotter and Thomspon's talent and ambition, Boyz II Men were the kings of CAPA in the late 1980s, with the boyz beating the Roots in CAPA's annual talent show.

In a 2014 interview with the *Huffington Post*, Black Thought and Questlove pointed to Boyz II Men's over-the-top showmanship as the deciding factor in their talent show victory.

"The talent shows were, like, huge, man. The production was an annual thing. They would call it Sentimental Journey. So, you know, it was all about who was performing at Sentimental Journey this year. Our rivals wound up being Boyz II Men," explained Black Thought.

"They used to cheat with glitter," Questlove

recalled. "Girls would start swooning. They would have glitter and the top hats."

During this late 1980s, CAPA was particularly talent-rich. Singer-songwriter Amel Larrieaux also attended the school before going on to rack up hit records with the smooth R&B duo Groove Theory and as a solo artist. In a 2012 interview with *Complex*, Larrieaux reflected on her time at CAPA and her classmates who'd reach stardom in the future.

"The two years I was there, Ahmir and Tariq from the Roots were there," she said. "Tariq was actually dating one of my close friends. Ahmir was there, Christian McBride, the bass player, was there, Joey DeFrancesco, all the guys from Boyz II Men, Marc Nelson—an original member of Boyz

II Men. And it's so funny because when I was at GFS [Germantown Friends School], I don't know if you know G-Love & Special Sauce, but Garrett and I were classmates as well. It's crazy, all of us that felt music—I was always singing choir, even at GFS, and performing in the talent show, and Garrett was doing his little band with his friends in his garage. But all of us really did follow through with our love for it, regardless of what journey or path we took."

When it was time to shoot the video for "Motownphilly," Boyz II Men even returned to CAPA and recruited their old classmate Questlove to make a cameo playing drums in the video. The song and video made great strides toward showing the world that CAPA was an incubator of talent.

CHAPTER 3

THE EAST COAST FAMILY

LEARNING FROM THE PAST

THE STORY OF HOW BOYZ II MEN MET MICHAEL Bivins as it was told on "Motownphilly" is obviously truncated and incomplete. After all, Bivins only had an eight-bar cameo. In the now-classic retelling, "four guys" from Philly "wanted to sing" so they approached Bivins. After singing a few expertly harmonized "dum-dum-da-da's," the rest is history.

◀ Michael Bivins performs in 1991.

▲ New Edition, circa 1970.

The full story is much richer and more nuanced. For Boyz II Men, Bivins' cosign didn't just offer a potential entryway into the music business. Bivins' approval brought the band into the orbit of their most significant influence, New Edition. In many ways, Boyz II Men were vying to pick up the mantle that Bivins' group once held as the most popular male vocal group in R&B. Winning him over gave the band a degree of legitimacy and positioned them as the next in line in a fraternity of male vocal groups who had put their stamp on R&B. To get a sense of why the Michael Bivins meeting was so important, we must first take a brief look at New Edition's history and their position as the reigning kings of R&B at the time.

Formed in 1978 in Boston and originally going by the name the Bricks, New Edition's members hailed from the largely Black and working-class neighborhood of Roxbury. The band's original members—Bobby Brown, Michael Bivins, Ricky Bell, Corey Rackney, and Travis Pettus—all grew up in the Orchard Park projects within close proximity to each other. The band initially came under the wing of Boston choreographer and manager Brooke Payne, who changed their name to the "New Edition of the Jackson 5," or New Edition for short. Rackney and Pettus eventually left the group and Ralph Tresvant and Payne's nephew, Ronnie DeVoe, replaced them.

The story goes that the group entered a talent competition called the Hollywood Talent Night, hosted at the Strand Theatre in Dorchester, another neighborhood in Boston. The show was run by nightlife proprietor Roscoe Gorham and Maurice Starr, a record producer and multi-instrumentalist from Boston. As author and Boston-born historian Dart Adams explains, "In Boston, the talent show circuit was akin to Texas high school football. We were that rabid about it, we were that into it because we were that good at it. The important thing to understand about New Edition is that they were kids, but they were competing against grownups in a lot of cases."

The group won a series of contests and was entered into the finals on November 15, 1981. That night, the group sang a Jackson 5 medley, paying homage to the group that they were modeling themselves after. Although New Edition came in second place that night and didn't go home with the $500 cash prize, they'd won something much more valuable: Starr's attention. The producer was looking for a group of young singers to get behind, saw an opportunity with the group, and approached them about working together. With New Edition and Starr working together, the band was poised to be the next big pop sensation, with infectious, danceable songs about young love, just like the Jackson 5 in the decade prior.

A preternaturally gifted, impeccably

▲ Poster art for
Candy Girl (1983).

choreographed band of young men, the Jackson 5 owned the 1960s. By 1978, tastes had changed, and the Jacksons had all grown up, leaving space for a new top boy band to emerge. The group's young prodigy, Michael, was about a year from releasing *Off The Wall*, his first "adult" album (thematically and literally), which would free him from the constraints of his past as a child star. Maurice Starr had a vision for New Edition to step into the void the Jacksons left behind.

> *By using hip-hop and electronic-style production as a sonic base, the trio of producers ensured that New Edition's sound would catch the ears of young people everywhere.*

New Edition's 1983 debut album, *Candy Girl*, is a remarkable time capsule of the era, full of bright synth- and drum machine-laced production from Starr, his brother Michael Jonzun, and "Planet Rock" producer Arthur Baker. At the time, Baker, Jonzun, and Starr were a red-hot production crew crafting undeniable hits for seminal hip-hop and dance labels like Sugar Hill, Tommy Boy, and Baker's own Streetwise and Partytime labels. By using hip-hop and electronic-style production as a sonic base, the trio of producers ensured that New Edition's sound would catch the ears of young people everywhere. When they took those cutting-edge hip-hop beats and melded them with accessible R&B melodies, they had a winning formula.

Candy Girl pulls direct inspiration from the lineage of male vocal groups that came before it with ballads like "Is This The End" and "Jealous Girl," which sound like 1980s reimaginings of late 1960s Motown hits. In addition to the Motown nods, *Candy Girl* is significant because it was one of the rare R&B full-lengths at the time to cede ground to the growing influence of hip-hop. The group included rapped verses in their songs and sonically, "Candy Girl," "Pass The Beat," and the album's opener, "Gimmie Your Love," were akin to the funky electro/hip-hop sounds being pioneered in the 1980s by Boston groups like Jonzun Crew and Planet Patrol.

In 1984, New Edition released their self-titled follow-up, which brought a refinement of the formula laid out on the first album. The ballads were still present, but two up-tempo singles from the album, "Cool It Now" and "Mr. Telephone Man," were smash hits that cemented New Edition's place as the top R&B group of the day and a pop-culture phenomenon. After initially dominating radio in Boston and up and down the East Coast, "Candy Girl" exploded nationally, with the song getting played on all the popular syndicated television dance shows of the day.

Author and historian Dart Adams was born and raised in Boston. In the 1980s, he knew the members of New Edition and saw the group's rise firsthand. "We started getting calls like 'Candy Girl' is going be on Casey Kasem's show," he said, explaining how surreal it was to see a group of local kids from the projects in Boston become superstars. "If you're watching *Solid Gold* and they play 'Candy Girl,' you're like, 'Wait a minute.' And people are dancing to 'Candy Girl' on *Soul Train*, they're dancing to it on *American Bandstand*."

The following year, 1985, saw the release of *All for Love*, and an event that would change the group forever: Bobby Brown left New Edition. In the years since, several reasons have been given to explain Brown's departure. But whether it was Brown's drug use, dissatisfaction with the music, or conflicts with management, it was clear that by losing its founding member, New Edition suffered a spiritual fracture that would not heal. While New Edition planned its next steps, Brown launched a wildly successful solo career beginning with the release of 1986's *King of Stage*.

New Edition followed Brown's exit with *Under the Blue Moon*, a retro-style album of covers full of faithful renditions of doo-wop classics like the Penguins' "Earth Angel" and "Tears On My Pillow" by Little Anthony and the Imperials. In 1987, the group recruited Washington, DC-born powerhouse singer Johnny Gill to replace Brown. While the group would return to form with the masterpiece *Heart Break*, the fissures in New Edition's foundation were irreparable. *Heart Break* was released in 1988, and New Edition would not last one year longer.

Many boy bands do not last long enough to mature in front of their audiences. While navigating financial strife with their label and internal issues, New Edition persevered, growing from adolescents into adulthood under the often-unforgiving public eye. While the group's talent-rich roster produced some great music during their time together, their personalities coupled with the pressures of fame and the industry made for a dynamic and caustic mix. The weight of years of vicious arguments, fistfights, drug abuse, and gunfights ended in their breakup in 1989.

When Michael Bivins met Boyz II Men, New Edition still existed in name, but the group had effectively fractured into two parts. Bivins, Ricky Bell, and Ronnie DeVoe were planning to defect and form the trio Bell Biv DeVoe, taking their hip-hop-informed sensibilities in their own direction. At Powerhouse II in Philly, Bell, Bivins, and DeVoe were set to announce the split from New Edition. It also seemed destined that Bivins and Boyz II Men would cross paths. The group auditioned for Bivins with "Can You Stand the Rain," a song choice that proved inspired, as they wowed everyone in the room. The audition convinced Bivins to give them his number so that they could talk further. Starting two weeks after exchanging numbers at Powerhouse, Nate Morris called Bivins every day for a month, talking about all things Boyz II Men. Eventually, Morris asked Bivins if he'd consider managing the group. In an interview at the 30th Annual NAMIC Conference at the 2016 NAMIC EMMA (Excellence in Multicultural Marketing Awards) Luncheon, Bivins explained how Morris' inquiry changed his perspective completely.

"[Nate] said, 'Everything you do in New Edition, you could do for us.' I said, 'Damn, I never thought of that,'" he remembered. "That was probably the best thing I could of did, was stop and listen. That moment there led me to change my life and my family's lives and it gave me an identity outside of the group. That kid, Nate Morris, believing in me helped me believe in myself."

> *"That was probably the best thing I could of did, was stop and listen. That moment there led me to change my life and my family's lives and it gave me an identity outside of the group. That kid, Nate Morris, believing in me helped me believe in myself."*

Having experienced the negative aspects of the artist's side of the music business, it made sense that Bivins would test his mettle as a manager and eventual label owner. New Edition famously clashed with their label over money, and at one point the band even returned home to Boston from a major tour with a few paltry $1.87 checks as compensation for their efforts. Having learned from the hard knocks of the music business, Bivins was savvy and now had the knowledge, personality, and drive to assume the role of strategist and mogul in the making. In the two years between that meeting in Philadelphia and the release of Boyz II Men's debut album, Bivins worked diligently to develop every aspect of the group's identity, sound, and presentation.

But even with Nate, Shawn, Michael, and Wanyá's talent and Bivins' knowledge of the business, the group still needed a label that would be willing to back the band.

> *Hip-hop, with its radical approach to sound, composition, performance, language, and social attitudes, represented a wholesale upheaval of the Black musical and cultural status quo.*

By 1989, Motown was primarily a legacy label. For most listeners, the Motown brand evoked images of the 1960s: meticulously coiffed girl groups and polished male vocalists cast in black-and-white video, singing the celebrated hits of a bygone era. While Motown was still beloved in the 1980s and early 1990s, the label was no longer hip, youthful, or progressive. Decades removed from their original releases, the Motown classics of the 1960s and early 1970s became fodder for nostalgia in the American popular consciousness. In 1983, *The Big Chill*, a film written and directed by Lawrence Kasdan, was released to great acclaim for its depiction of changing adult friendships—and its Motown-packed soundtrack. Like many pieces of popular media from the time, *The Big Chill* highlighted Motown's music for its "feel good" quality. Without the Civil Rights Movement and social unrest that inspired them, rebellious protest songs like Marvin Gaye's "What's Going On" and Martha and the Vandellas' "Dancing in the Street" became quaint oldies. By 1988, the Barrett Strong and Norman Whitfield-penned classic "Heard It Through the Grapevine," a raw, aching story of infidelity, was being used in television commercials to sell California raisins.

It wasn't just nostalgia that pushed Motown from the cutting edge of Black music during this time. Hip-hop, with its radical approach to sound, composition, performance, language, and social attitudes, represented a wholesale

▲ Boyz II Men, circa 1990.

▶ Boyz II Men with members of the Jackson family in 1992.

upheaval of the Black musical and cultural status quo. While the music had clear and identifiable ties to the past and older musical traditions, hip-hop made the very idea of Motown seem old school. Though stars like Rick James, Dennis Edwards, and Teena Marie released brilliant records for the label in the 1980s, by the end of the decade, Motown was in desperate need of some new blood. Even Michael Jackson, the biggest star the label had produced, had long since moved on from Motown, releasing his record-breaking 1980s albums on Epic.

Just as the Jackson 5 and Motown had inspired Bivins during the early New Edition days, the label would once again provide direction for the next chapter in his career. Upon signing Boyz II Men with Motown,

Bivins and the label's then-president, Jheryl Busby, recruited Dallas Austin to handle production for the group's debut album, *Cooleyhighharmony*. A young, skillful musician living in Atlanta, Austin had racked up credits on records from Californian R&B outfit Troop and the Prince-inspired funk group Princess & Starbreeze before he turned twenty-one. Although Boyz II Men and Austin eventually fell out (Austin referred to the group as "assholes" in a 2020 interview with the YouTube channel VladTV), the pairing was a stroke of genius in 1990. With hip-hop and its youthful energy emerging as the primary cultural force in Black America, any R&B act hoping to make waves in the market had to incorporate it into their sound.

By 1990, hip-hop had become such an omnipresent influence in Black music, even older acts like Stevie Wonder and Earth, Wind & Fire were incorporating rap and hip-hop-style beats into their new music. If Motown and Bivins had opted to hire an older, more experienced producer to work with Boyz II Men, they may not have been able to concoct their modern, cutting-edge sound. Worse yet, an older producer may have opted to lean too heavily into the band's doo-wop and Motown influences and created an album full of retro-styled tracks. Austin instead brought the power and texture of hip-hop beats and married it with the musicality of R&B.

This winning formula did not end with Boyz II Men. Relying on his ear and reputation as a hit-maker, Bivins set about building a stable of artists dubbed "The East Coast Family" who would all play with their own poppy mixture of hip-hop and R&B. Alongside Boyz II Men, Bivins was developing the Atlanta-based prepubescents Another Bad Creation, MC Brains (who scored a hit in 1991 with "Oochie Coochie"), the rapper Tam Rock, and the teenage band Sudden Impact. With Bivins adding his input to his artists' sounds as well as their looks and choreography, members of the East Coast Family got the kind of all-encompassing artist development that is just not available to many young artists today. Bivins likely learned this kind of comprehensive approach from his time working with Maurice Starr in the early New Edition days, but it was nothing new. Berry Gordy had done it with the Jackson 5, and it was similar to what Brian Epstein had done with the Beatles. Although the East Coast Family's existence as a proper collective was short-lived, they did release a compilation album, *The East Coast Family Vol. 1*, in 1992. A joint venture between Motown and Bivins' newly launched Biv10 imprint, the album featured the entire roster of acts signed to Bivins' label and a handful of remixes of Boyz II Men songs "Motownphilly," "It's So Hard To Say Goodbye To Yesterday," and "Sympin'." Many of the acts in Bivins' stable didn't make much of an impact critically or on the charts with the obvious exception of Boyz II Men and ABC, the latter of which had two bona fide hit singles, "Iesha" in 1990 and "Playground" in 1991. But Michael Bivins had an ace in the hole in Boyz II Men, and their debut album would more than justify Bivins' and Motown's time and investment.

DALLAS AUSTIN AND ATLANTA'S HIP-HOP TAKEOVER

TODAY, ATLANTA, GEORGIA, IS RIGHTFULLY RECOGNIZED AS A CREATIVE AND COMMERCIAL EPICENTER OF HIP-HOP MUSIC. IN THE GENRE'S FIRST TWO DECADES—BETWEEN 1973 AND 1993— THAT WAS NOT THE CASE, AS NEW YORK HELD ONTO ITS TITLE AS THE GENRE'S MOST INFLUENTIAL CITY.

While Atlanta has produced plenty of stars and notable acts, Dallas Austin is a key figure in the story of the city's ascent. While landmark albums like Outkast's *ATLiens* and Goodie Mob's *Soul Food* stand among some of the best of the 1990s, it wasn't until the 2000s that the city would make a serious case for itself as hip-hop's new capital city. Riding a wave of anthemic hits by artists like Usher, Lil Jon, Ludacris, and T.I., the 2000s saw Atlanta solidify its place as a major incubator of Black music's biggest talents.

A decade before Atlanta's wholesale take-over of the charts, Dallas Austin paved the way for Atlanta to become a top hip-hop city. Born in Columbus, Georgia, in 1970, Austin possessed grand ambitions at a young age. A gifted multi-in-strumentalist, Austin taught himself to play music by listening to songs on the radio and playing along on his Casio keyboard. At thirteen, his dream of

becoming a world-famous musician brought him to Atlanta. Seeing how determined her son was to make it in the music business, Austin's mom sold her restaurant and made the trip with him.

By the time he was sixteen, Austin was working as a writer and producer, racking up credits on albums by Prince-inspired R&B act Princess & Starbreeze and the popular male vocal group Troop. His breakout as a producer came in 1990, with the release of Another Bad Creation's high-energy puppy-love anthem, "Iesha." Discovered by Michael Bivins, the Atlanta boys' quintet combined the energy of hip-hop with R&B, via Austin's frenetic production. Reaching No. 9 on the *Billboard* Hot 100 chart and No. 6 on the R&B chart, "Iesha" and its follow-up single, "Playground," were ubiquitous on Black radio in 1990. Between 1991 and 1992, Austin also scored massive hits with TLC's "Ain't 2 Proud 2 Beg" and of course, Boyz II Men's "Motownphilly."

In a 2019 interview with Billboard, Austin talked about the process of creating "Motownphilly" and how his chemistry with the group led to him working on *Cooleyhighharmony*. "With 'Motownphilly,' the guys came up with the title and I didn't get it at first because I was in Atlanta. But then when I went to work with them in Philly, I got it, and it was really fun writing the song from there." Austin worked on a song or two with the group, then asked if he could do the whole album. The group hoped to work with a more established producer, like Babyface or Jimmy Jam and Terry Lewis. As Austin explained, "I went back to the hotel and started listening to Babyface albums and I listened to Jimmy and Terry, and I went back into the studio with them and I said, 'Look, I can make these songs.'" After three songs, the group agreed.

Throughout the 1990s, many classic songs were marked by Austin's prowess as a songwriter and producer. Alongside DJ/producer Jermaine Dupri, Babyface, and L.A. Reid, Austin was part of a small cadre of hitmakers making a significant impression on the national charts and the sound of Black popular music. As homegrown artists and producers like Dupri, T.I., Gucci Mane, Lil Jon, and others burned up the charts in the 2000s, the pendulum of hip-hop swung in Atlanta's direction.

In the fantastic 2023 NPR Music piece "How Atlanta Became the Center of the Rap Universe," writer Jewel Wicker eloquently described Atlanta as "the center of the rap universe, the last semblance of a monoculture." Today, Atlanta remains at the forefront of Black popular music, and it's hard to imagine the city rising to the status it now enjoys without the groundwork laid by Dallas Austin.

▲ Dallas Austin receives the Legends of Atlanta Award as a community leader on the Atlanta music scene in 2008.

CHAPTER 4

COOLEYHIGH-HARMONY

CREATING MUSIC THAT CROSSED GENERATIONS

A S FAR AS DEBUT ALBUMS GO, BOYZ II Men's *Cooleyhighharmony* is as indebted to the past as it was cutting edge. Combining Take 6 and doo-wop-influenced vocal harmony with classic R&B balladry, plus a few nods to contemporary hip-hop and New Jack Swing production, the album was a culmination of multiple strains of Black music culture and history. This eclecticism did not happen by accident.

◄ Boyz II Men perform at Summer Jam 1991 in Mountain View, California, in August 1991.

Through the musical influence of their families and the community around them, as well as their training at CAPA, the band was well versed in a wide variety of older Black musical styles and performance techniques. As they would display throughout *Cooleyhighharmony* in 1991, Boyz II Men were not a retro act.

Shawn, Wanyá, Nate, and Michael were four young men coming of age as hip-hop reached for greater commercial and creative heights. When hip-hop culture first began to form in the early 1970s, it was the most revolutionary cultural movement to come out of the post–Civil Rights era. Rap music and the hip-hop culture that produced it were fundamentally unruly, and damn near everything that hip-hop's first generation did was deemed highly unconventional by the rest of the world. As the defining American youth culture of its day, hip-hop broke and reformed established social, musical, and cultural norms with abandon. Despite hip-hop's often reckless desire to push things forward, it could be argued that it was the culture's obsession with the past that made a group like Boyz II Men and an album like *Cooleyhighharmony* possible in the first place.

When *Cooleyhighharmony* was released in the spring of 1991, Black youth culture was in the midst of a renaissance that was being felt in film, fashion, visual art, and, of course, music. The jazz-tinged rap music of

the Native Tongues (an early 1990s collective that included A Tribe Called Quest, De La Soul, Queen Latifah, the Jungle Brothers, and more) helped open the world up to the possibilities of a new Black bohemia. This particular strain of late 1980s/early 1990s rap dovetailed beautifully with a wave of Black cultural and political consciousness that swept through the US at the time. Black kids in cities around the country were embracing Afrocentricity, an academic theory created by Dr. Molefi Asante that centers the experiences of African people and the African diaspora within their own cultural, historical, and sociological contexts. Many embraced the philosophies and iconography of historical Black freedom fighters like Malcolm X, Marcus Garvey, and Assata Shakur. By tapping into the Black radical tradition and its figureheads from the past, Black youth were able to draw a connection between their struggle against poverty, systemic racism, police brutality, the apartheid regime in South Africa, and the political battles that their forebearers fought.

Just as Black youth in this era looked back to the 1960s and 1970s for political inspiration, hip-hop music sought lessons from the past through the art of sampling. Technological advancements in the 1980s came right on time, as hip-hop producers scoured record bins for material to sample. Early 1990s rap classics like A Tribe Called Quest's *The Low*

End Theory, De La Soul's *Buhloone Mindstate*, and Diamond D & the Psychotic Neurotic's *Stunts Blunts & Hip-Hop* were vibrant collages of jazz, funk, soul, blues, and rock records from the 1960s and 1970s. The interest in older music generated by hip-hop helped to create a mass dialogue between Black baby boomers and Gen X. This dialogue and cultural exchange helped set an atmosphere of openness that allowed four hip-hop adjacent, doo-wop-schooled kids from Philly to create an album that would bridge these seemingly disparate sounds and the generational gap.

> *Just as Black youth in this era looked back to the 1960s and 1970s for political inspiration, hip-hop music sought lessons from the past through the art of sampling.*

In a further bid to conjure nostalgic memories of the past, Boyz II Men chose a peculiar title for their debut full-length: *Cooleyhighharmony*. Written by Eric Monte and directed by Michael Schultz, the film *Cooley High* was an established classic in Black households by the time Boyz II Men referenced it for their album. Oddly enough, though *Cooley High* was originally released in 1975, the film was already a work of nostalgia by 1991. Set in Chicago in 1964, *Cooley High*'s screenplay was based on the life experiences of a teenage Monte and his group of friends. The slang, the fashion, and the evocative sounds of Motown made the film a hit among audiences seeking to relive the halcyon days of the 1960s. For Boyz II Men, a film depicting the lives of a group of ambitious young Black boys growing up in the inner city and surrounded by the sounds of 1960s soul was the perfect cultural touchstone to reference with their debut. The group's members were all in their late teens and early twenties when they chose to name their album after *Cooley High* and likely felt a sort of kinship to the main characters and their struggles.

In the early 1990s, Studio 4 was an institution in Philly's music scene. While the studio has since moved outside the city limits to a small Schuylkill River-bordering suburb called Conshohocken, it remains crucial to the fabric of Philadelphia music culture. Founded in 1980 by audio engineers and twin brothers Phil Nicolo and Joe "The Butcher" Nicolo, Studio 4 was initially built at 3rd and Callowhill in Philly's Northern Liberties neighborhood. The studio scored early hits, recording 1980s rockers like the Hooters, Lita Ford, dance-poppers Pretty Poison, and a generation of Philly hip-hop legends like Schoolly D, Steady B, Cool C, and Three Times Dope. In the summer of 1987, the Nicolos entered into a partnership with Philly manager/record promoter/jack-of-all-trades Chris Schwartz to branch out and create Ruffhouse Records, one of the most commercially successful hip-hop labels of the 1990s. Eventually, Ruffhouse's roster swelled, producing massive, multimillion-selling acts like Cypress Hill, Kris Kross, the Fugees, Lauryn Hill, and more. When Boyz II Men began the sessions for *Cooleyhighharmony*, Ruffhouse was on fire and Studio 4 was as hot as any studio in the country.

Joe Nicolo recalled how Boyz II Men came to record *Cooleyhighharmony* at Studio 4 and made the record with one of the studio's young engineers: "Jim 'Jiff' Hinger, he actually was an assistant engineer at Studio 4. And there was this project coming in, it wasn't really a record yet but it was a demo from Motown. And we said 'Jiff, you wanna take on the project?' And he's like 'I'd love to!' It was his first real project. He became their engineer and worked with them for years after that."

Cooleyhighharmony was recorded in about six weeks in 1991, and the group covered a lot of ground in that short amount of time. In a 2016 interview with *Wax Poetics*, producer Dallas Austin gave insight into why the album was produced and recorded so quickly, saying, "Once 'Motownphilly' came out, it started to take off, so we had to hurry up and get the album done."

Austin also walked the *Wax Poetics* interviewer through the process of producing the album's tracks. "The first thing I would do is lay down the drums," he explained. "I had so many drum loops going on at the same time. This was before clearances came. [laughs] Then, I would play a regular bass line in a regular song on top of all these loops that were out of tune. And some kind of way it would come together. I used to like listening to the Bomb Squad and Public Enemy. By the time I got the bass and keys down and the roots of it down, then everything else would fill in around it. Back then, I used to use a lot of horns. It was the start of New Jack Swing and the swing era. That was Teddy Riley's influence."

The group recorded in Studio 4's A room, often with Austin seated at the keyboard, writing with the group or working out arrangements. To finish the album quickly, the group would often begin a session in the afternoon and work past midnight. Despite the time constraints, *Cooleyhighharmony* is

◄ Boyz II Men attend the *Billboard* Music Awards in December 1991.

▶ Dallas Austin, producer of Boyz II Men's debut album, Cooleyhighharmony.

a markedly strong and polished body of work, practically overflowing with impassioned lead performances and rich vocal harmonies. The quartet's vocal talent is the centerpiece and driving force of each song. A myriad of Black vocal traditions are put on full display, as the band incorporates gospel-style runs, jazz harmonies and phrasing, doo-wop, and hip-hop into a contemporary R&B package. Above all, *Cooleyhighharmony* speaks to the power and lasting vitality of ensemble singing in the age of hip-hop. More than a mere update of the great balladeers of the 1960s, 1970s, and 1980s, Boyz II Men came out the gate swinging on their first album, making a strong case for why older forms of Black vocal performance were still relevant in a contemporary context.

"Nate, Shawn, and I did the core of the writing," Dallas Austin explained to *Wax Poetics*. "They would have harmony arrangements, and I would come back in and rearrange them to make them fuller and make them into different parts that would go on top of each other. Nate and Shawn spearheaded the writing and how the melodies would sound on songs."

The album opens with "Please Don't Go," a gorgeous Nate-penned ballad and desperate plea to save a relationship. Backed by an acoustic guitar and pizzicato strings, the song's achingly paced tempo reflects the yearning of the lyrics. Michael opens the tune with one of his signature spoken interludes, offering his partner a simple, "Hey, baby, I'm sorry. I never meant to hurt you," an apology that is either ineffectively earnest or inappropriately cheeky. Following the song's famous "Nayhoo" ad-lib, the quartet swells in unison, washing the song in glorious harmonies. Shawn takes the lead verses, his voice wrapping around the vocal melody subtly without over-singing.

> *"Nate and Shawn spearheaded the writing and how the melodies would sound on songs."*

In the 1994 promotional documentary *Then II Now*, the band returned to CAPA to meet with David King and his latest crop of students. Surrounded by students and with Nate seated at the piano, the group perform a stripped-down version of "Please Don't Go" that only reinforces the song's musical and emotional depth. In an interview in the documentary, Shawn gives insight into the arrangement process and how he came to sing lead on "Please Don't Go."

"The guys come to me when something

needs to be sang smooth and soft and mellow because I guess that's the way I like to sing and that's the way I like to hear singers sing," he explained. "I like to get into people who sing a song with and controls it with gentleness."

Nate takes over the lead for the pre-chorus and ups the emotional ante dramatically. The chorus relieves the tension built by the previous verses and pre-chorus, leaving us with naked, unabashed desire. The desire that propels "Please Don't Go" is not carnal—that'll come later in the album—but a desire to reconcile and salvage love, a set of emotions that get to the core of what R&B is. Sex and infatuation are important and ever-present in the genre, but the desire to hold on to love in spite of all life's travails is the emotional force that animates R&B.

Listeners are thrown deeper into the well of romantic love and loss with the album's second track, "Lonely Heart." Like "Please Don't Go," Nate is credited as the song's writer, and Michael opens the song with a monologue, though this time an uncredited woman plays his counterpart. Nate and Shawn alternate leads, then dovetail beautifully for the final line of the verse where we realize that the love is gone and the relationship is over. "This Is My Heart" completes a trilogy of similarly constructed ballads with its slow, relaxed tempo, polished musical arrangement, and lyrics that find the band on the verge of losing love. "Uhh

Ahh" immediately offers a change in tone and energy beginning with its jazzy "ten, nine, eight, seven . . ." countdown. The wordless grunts and moans of the chorus take us out of the ecstatic heights of romantic love and drag us deep into the primal realm of sex and physicality. Released as the third single from *Cooleyhighharmony* behind "Motownphilly" and "Under Pressure," "Uhh Ahh" was clearly positioned to offer a counterbalance to the squeaky clean and preppy image that the band established in the "Motownphilly" video. Drenched in reverb with a velvety backing track, the song seems designed to fit into the quiet storm syndicated Black radio format that prioritized smooth jazz and romantic R&B ballads.

In a thematically curious choice of song sequencing, "Uhh Ahh" is immediately followed by "It's So Hard To Say Goodbye To Yesterday," a highlight of Boyz II Men's live performances in those early years. The song is a cover of the G. C. Cameron song from 1975, co-written by husband-and-wife duo Freddie Perren and Christine Yarian for *Cooley High*. "It's So Hard . . ." closes the film on a somber, heart-wrenching note, Cameron's version ripe with instrumentation in the form of gospel-inspired organ, piano, strings, and brass. Boyz II Men strip away all the original musical arrangement, getting to the heart of the emotion and truth of the song with their

minimalist, a cappella version. Their voices are the only instruments present on the track. In the hands of Boyz II Men, Perren and Yarian's winding, sorrowful melody is treated with care and real emotional honesty. It's a profoundly sad song, but it conjures no feeling of defeat or hopelessness.

> "Once the mixing of that record was done, I remember the band being like, 'I don't know, man, but those rough mixes that we have on cassette, they still bang.'"

For music fans who bought their copy of *Cooleyhighharmony* on cassette or vinyl LP, the album was divided into two sides, each reflecting the sound and energy of the songs they contained. Side A was dubbed "Adagio," an Italian phrase denoting a piece of music performed at a slow tempo while Side B was the "Allegro" side or songs performed at a brisk, lively tempo. Naturally, "Motownphilly" opens the second half of the album, swinging for the fences with its up-tempo production and dense, hectic arrangement. "Under Pressure" follows, opening with a recording of the group practicing a peppy, classic doo-wop-style a cappella. Producer Dallas Austin suggests they switch things up a bit musically and the group agrees; the chunky, New Jack Swing-influenced beat for "Under Pressure" hits, pushing the energy back up to ten. Occupying the same sonic universe as Austin's production on TLC's *Oooooooohhh... On the TLC Tip*, "Under Pressure" takes a collage-like approach, with multiple samples layered on top of one another, including a Flavor Flav vocal sample that hints at the influence of the Bomb Squad, the production team behind Public Enemy's trademark wall of noise/kitchen sink-style beats. The song's busy, layered production, coupled with Nate's lyrics about a young man in desperate pursuit of a young woman, makes the song a fun experiment.

Like the other up-tempo songs on the album, "Under Pressure" and the James Brown and James Bond score-sampling "Sympin'" are solid but mostly remind us why ballads were the band's strength, especially in those early days. One quality shared by both the up-tempo songs and the ballads on *Cooleyhighharmony* is the quality of the vocal performances. "Sympin'," "Under Pressure," and "Motownphilly" are harmonic wonders, with the group melding four-man vocal parts with booming hip-hop beats to stunning effect. The complexity and power of the vocals throughout the album are more shocking when you consider the ages of the group's members at the time. None of them were older than twenty-two when their debut album hit the streets. Their skill was uncommon and likely the product of years of woodshedding and training at CAPA.

But once the fully mixed version of the album made it back to Jheryl Busby at Motown, a problem presented itself. Both Busby and the group decided that they were not completely happy with the final product. Throughout the recording process, a series of rough mixes of the songs had been made that weren't intended to make it onto the album.

As Joe Nicolo explained, "Once the mixing of that record was done, I remember the band being like, 'I don't know, man, but those rough mixes that we have on cassette, they still bang. We just love the way those mixes sound, simple, a little bit of reverb on the vocals. We just really like those mixes.' Half of those records are just those reference mixes from the Neve console."

Upon its release on April 30, 1991, the album debuted at No. 58 on the US *Billboard* 200, but it eventually ascended to No. 3, as well as earning a peak position of No. 1 on the R&B/Hip-Hop Albums chart. Although it was just the group's opening shot, *Cooleyhighharmony* would set a new standard for R&B vocal performance. Commercially, it was also a massive hit. While "Motownphilly" proved to be an effective introduction and early selling point for the album, the band still needed to hit the road and win over new crowds. Their first major tour the following year would bring a number of opportunities that would change Boyz II Men's trajectory.

U KNOW

"I remember it like it was yesterday. In 1991, my older sister bought the *Cooleyhighharmony* album. I was ten years old at the time. My favorite feature on the boombox was 'repeat' because I loved playing certain songs over and over at bedtime. The whole album was great, but 'Please Don't Go' and 'Uhh Ahh' were my favorites to wear out." —*Iman Williams, fan*

THE BOYZ GOT STYLE

IN THEIR NUMEROUS RED CARPET APPEARANCES AND SPECIAL PERFORMANCES, BOYZ II MEN HAVE ESTABLISHED A SPECIFIC "LOOK" THROUGH THEIR FASHION.

They often pair preppy with casual, wearing blazers and ties with jeans and a baseball cap. And since the 1990s were all about oversized, you better believe that those blazers landed mid-thigh on the bottom and an inch past their wrists on the sleeves. *GQ* calls them the unsung heroes of the "preppy revolution."

Whether the look was a blazer and a cap, an oversized windbreaker and khaki shorts, or a sequin blue sweater with a bowtie, the Boyz were almost always matching at appearances in their peak. This was all from the mind of their music manager Michael Bivins, founding member of New Edition.

"We weren't really into it at first," Shawn told *GQ*. "But once we started wearing the stuff and learning how to put it together, it started to feel good."

During their 2013 Las Vegas residency at the Mirage, Boyz II Men sported a look that was a little bit different. Having aged out of their preppy, college-boy look, the Boyz took a mature approach, decked out in white from head to toe. There's still an element of casualness, with a sleek blazer paired with high-top sneakers and a plain T-shirt, but overall the all-white gives an air of opulence and sophistication.

▶ Boyz II Men show off their style in 1992.

CHAPTER 5

END OF THE ROAD

TRIUMPH AND TRAGEDY ON TOUR

N A MOVE THAT SOLIDIFIED THEM AS an emerging presence in pop music, Boyz II Men embarked on their first major tour in 1992, hitting the road with MC Hammer, the hottest artist in music at the time. More than three decades removed from MC Hammer's commercial peak, it may be hard for younger music fans to understand just how big and impactful the rapper/dancer was.

◄ The group in Germany in 1992.

Born Stanley Kirk Burrell in Oakland in 1962, when Hammer's major label debut, *Let's Get It Started*, was released by Capitol Records in the fall of 1988, hip-hop was in the midst of a golden era. Now recognized as one of the greatest twelve-month periods in rap music history, 1988 was marked by the release of genre-defining classics like N.W.A.'s "Straight Outta Compton," Slick Rick's "The Great Adventures Of Slick Rick," and Public Enemy's *It Takes A Nation Of Millions To Hold Us Back*, with rappers, DJs, and producers mining new and previously uncharted lyrical, sonic, and emotional depths. Not only had the music grown in complexity, rap music artists were making great strides commercially. Far removed from the parks and rec centers of the South Bronx, hip-hop had proven that it was capable of attracting audiences outside its immediate cultural orbit.

This was the landscape upon which MC Hammer landed, and he was ready to take up the mantle of the genre's next crossover pop star. Propelled by the triumvirate of hit singles "Let's Get It Started," "Turn This Mutha Out," and "(Hammer Hammer) They Put Me In The Mix," "Let's Get It Started" stormed the charts, eventually selling over three million copies. If "Let's Get It Started" was the Trojan horse, 1990's massive hit, *Please Hammer Don't Hurt 'Em* was MC Hammer's most concerted and effective assault on the mainstream. Having sold an estimated seventeen million copies worldwide to date, *Please Hammer Don't Hurt 'Em* remains one of the highest-selling rap albums of all time. The album's centerpiece was the Rick James-sampling single, "U Can't Touch This." A slick update of James' funk-new wave hybrid "Super Freak" from 1981, "U Can't Touch This" not only ruled radio and video music programming hubs like BET, MTV, and VH1, the song also permeated pop cultural consciousness like no rap song before it. In the course of a year, "U Can't Touch This" leaped from the charts into nearly every facet of pop culture, from TV references on shows like Fox's *In Living Color* to countless bootleg T-shirts throughout the country. Like any true pop-culture phenomenon, the wave of "Hammermania" that briefly took hold in the early 1990s was far-reaching and seemingly inescapable. As Burrell's music dominated the charts, he also made guest appearances and performances on TV and appeared in advertisements selling KFC popcorn chicken. Toy manufacturing juggernaut Mattel produced an MC Hammer Ken doll, and in the fall of 1991, ABC began airing *Hammerman*, a Saturday

◄ MC Hammer in 1992.

▲ Boyz II Men
photographed in 1992.

morning cartoon show in which Burrell used a pair of magical dancing shoes to fight a rogues' gallery of wacky supervillains.

Boyz II Men found themselves aligned with Hammer's titanic wave of mainstream success in 1992. In March of that year, the group joined Hammer as an opening act for his highly anticipated Too Legit To Quit World Tour. To get a sense of the scale of the tour, Hammer began by selling out the fifty-thousand-capacity Tokyo Dome before embarking on a 100+ city tour across the United States, Canada, Mexico, and Asia. In the November 3, 2001, issue of *Billboard* magazine, Nate recalled, "When we were on our first tour with MC Hammer, we were doing three to four songs. As we went along, we started to see more people who recognized us. Then the venue starts to fill up a lot more in the early stages of the tour. That actually forced Hammer to give us more songs. 'It's So Hard To Say Goodbye To Yesterday' came out during that tour. Then the video hit MTV. It actually got to the point where Hammer had to readjust on the financial end. He realized how much of the audience we were actually bringing in."

After a twenty-one-day stint throughout the American South, on April 22, 1992, the Too Legit To Quit Tour arrived in Boyz II Men's hometown of Philadelphia. The concert was held at the Spectrum, the legendary—and now demolished—South Philly

arena. The eighteen-thousand-capacity venue was perfect for the bold spectacle that Hammer brought to town. Armed with a full band, a battery of dancers, and a full choir, Hammer's live presentation took hip-hop to its most grandiose extremes.

In a scathing *Daily News* review, journalist Jonathan Takiff largely panned Hammer's Philadelphia performance, dismissing the ambitious show as a "circus" and calling it "heavy-handed." Despite his dissatisfaction with the Hammer-led portion of the show, Takiff praised Boyz II Men's live performances of "It's So Hard To Say Goodbye" and "Motownphilly" as "sharply harmonized" and "well received."

In May 1992, an unexpected tragedy struck while the group was riding the high of life on the road for their first big tour. On May 25, Boyz II Men's road manager, Roderick Khalil Rountree, was shot and killed following a concert at the Rosemont Horizon (now Allstate Center) in Chicago. Described as "a father figure" in a public statement issued by the group after his death, Rountree provided a mature guiding influence over the band of young men navigating fame and the task of growing up in the public eye. At thirty-six years old, Rountree was a music business veteran who'd racked up twenty years of experience in the industry by 1992. In addition to his work with groups like the Manhattans, Harold Melvin & the

► The group poses with Khalil Rountree in 1989.

Blue Notes, and New Edition, Rountree was described by Ricky Bell in a 2017 Instagram tribute as "the bodyguard who kept us in line."

In an interview for *Then II Now*, Wanyá said of Rountree, "He played a big part in our lives. He taught us all kinds of things. In many ways, we relied on Khalil. When God took Khalil away . . . when it happened, it was kind of like we had to learn how to fly on our own."

> *"When God took Khalil away . . . when it happened, it was kind of like we had to learn how to fly on our own."*

Following the show at the Rosemont, the group and their entourage were staying at the Guest Quarters Suites Hotel in Chicago's Gold Coast neighborhood. Around 5 a.m. an altercation broke out between Rountree and three men, Christopher Babbington, Chris Foley, and Kenneth Copeland. Rountree's friend and Boyz II Men's assistant road manager and head of security, Qadree El-Amin, was also shot in the knee during the altercation.

In court transcripts from the Appellate Court of Illinois, First District, Second Division, case of *People v. Babbington*, El-Amin gives a harrowing account of the night of the fatal shooting:

"El-Amin testified that the defendant was wearing an expression like 'nothing is happening.' The decedent appeared to be scared and said, 'These guys was trying to break in my room, what do you all want, what do you all want?' El-Amin said, 'Let's take 'em downstairs to security.' El-Amin stepped into the elevator. As the doors closed, defendant's expression changed 'to more of a suspicious-type person.' El-Amin testified that the defendant and the other two men charged at him and the decedent. During the ensuing scuffle, El-Amin saw sparks fly from the defendant's direction and heard three gunshots, but did not see a gun."

Understandably shocked and shaken by Rountree's murder, the band took a break from the tour to grieve and refocus. In an interview with the *Des Moines Register* in 2019, reflecting on Rountree's death, Nathan revealed that it took time for the band to heal and move on: "When [Rountree] was killed in Chicago, it turned us upside down for a while."

Despite the deep personal turmoil and

confusion following the tragic and senseless death of Rountree, the band still managed to work while taking a hiatus from the tour. On the eve of their return to the road, Boyz II Men recorded the song that would go on to be their biggest and most enduring hit. "End Of The Road" was composed by the legendary song-writing duo of Daryl Simmons and Kenneth "Babyface" Edmonds. Written on a rainy day at a lowkey home studio in Atlanta, "End Of The Road" was created for the soundtrack to the 1992 film, *Boomerang*. The Reginald Hudlin-directed, Eddie Murphy-helmed romantic comedy focused on the love lives of a handful of young Black professionals living in New York City. Executive produced by Babyface and his business partner, Antonio "L.A." Reid, *Boomerang*'s soundtrack was stacked with future classics from some of R&B's best. While Toni Braxton's bittersweet kiss-off "Love Shoulda Brought You Home" and PM Dawn's ethereal love ballad "I'd Die Without You" were standouts, "End Of The Road" would prove to be the album's flagship hit, breaking chart records and propelling Boyz II Men into mainstream stardom.

A grand and emotionally wrought portrait of a relationship in the process of collapse, "End Of The Road" was released after Boyz II

▲ Kenneth "Babyface" Edmonds in 1992.

Men rejoined the Too Legit to Quit World Tour, ascending the charts while the group worked on the road. With Wanyá, Nate, and Shawn alternating on lead vocals, the song journeys through the pain and outright desperation of men trying to hold on to a lover who doesn't want to be held. The big, earth-shattering harmonies on the chorus act as a release valve for all the pressure and tension built up throughout the verses.

> *"You can't ask for anything more from a song. It's developed an immortality. We want to have those types of records that will outlive us."*

Speaking with SongwriterUniverse.com years later, Daryl Simmons recalled the process of writing "End Of The Road" in Atlanta, then quickly recording it with the group in Philadelphia right before they went back on tour: "We needed a song for Boyz II Men—they agreed to do the soundtrack. Kenny had bought a house in Buckhead just for us to work on music. So we drive down there. I'll never forget it . . . it was a rainy, awful day. Kenny's there—we knew we had to come up with this song. So he starts going through some ideas.

In between, we took a break and played this little hockey game. Then Kenny goes back, and he kind of hits on these chords. At the time, Kenny had been through a divorce, and I was going through a divorce. So here we go with this concept, thinking about [how things were at] the end of the road.

"Then we jump on a plane to Philadelphia, because the next night Boyz II Men are leaving for a tour. We arrive at the studio. I think Shawn comes in, and says, 'We've got a problem.' We ask, 'What's that?' 'Wanyá has no voice. He's been singing so hard for this tour, he has no voice.' We say, 'Okay, we'll give him a night's rest . . . we'll come back tomorrow.' Shawn says, 'No, we leave in the morning [for the tour].' So Wanyá says, 'I can probably sing it, but I've gotta stand way back in the corner of the room, and just sing it as loud as I can.'" Wanyá battled through, the song was mixed, and "End Of The Road" was born.

On August 15, 1992, "End Of The Road" hit No. 1 on the *Billboard* Hot 100 chart. The band was set to perform in New Haven, Connecticut, that night, unaware that the majestic ballad they had just released was primed to break a three-decade-old record set by none other than Elvis Presley. For the next thirteen weeks, "End Of The Road" sat atop the *Billboard* Hot 100, breaking the record set by Elvis back in 1956 with "Hound Dog/Don't Be

Cruel." The band was across the pond, touring in London, when they got word that they had broken Elvis' record.

Today, "End Of The Road" enjoys a firm standing among the most important R&B ballads of all time. The breakup song to end all breakup songs, "End Of The Road" not only perfectly communicated the passion and hurt that has fueled great R&B songs for decades, but its power and memorability made it a hit across multiple demographics. On November 14, "End Of The Road" was finally knocked out of the No. 1 spot by "How Do You Talk To An Angel" by the Heights, the fictional band at the center of *The Heights*, a new Fox young adult drama.

In a 2022 *New York Post* article, the group playfully suggested that audiences would boo them today if they removed "End Of The Road" from their live setlist. Rather than feel encumbered by fans' love for the decades-old hit, Shawn is appreciative of the song's longevity. "You can't ask for anything more from a song," he told the *Post*. "It's developed an immortality. We want to have those types of records that will outlive us."

Hoping to capitalize on the song's success, Motown released a special edition of *Cooleyhighharmony* that included "End Of The Road." Beyond the accolades, awards, and record sales, "End Of The Road" would go on to achieve something much more significant. As the go-to song for countless graduations and funerals over the years, the song has become part of our cultural lexicon.

With the success of the Too Legit Tour and the chart dominance of "End Of The Road," Boyz II Men were poised to ascend to a new stratum of fame and notoriety. Riding a massive wave of momentum, the band entered 1993 on the verge of becoming one of the biggest pop acts of the decade.

REMEMBERING
KHALIL ROUNTREE SR.

RODERICK KHALIL ROUNTREE WAS A FAMILY MAN AND A VETERAN OF THE ENTERTAINMENT BUSINESS. NOT ONLY DID HE WORK WITH CELEBRATED MUSICAL ACTS LIKE HAROLD MELVIN & THE BLUE NOTES, NEW EDITION, AND BOYZ II MEN, ROUNTREE WAS ALSO A PERSONAL BODYGUARD FOR MUHAMMAD ALI. FOLLOWING HIS TRAGIC DEATH IN 1992, HIS FRIENDS, FAMILY, AND COLLEAGUES FOUGHT TO KEEP HIS MEMORY ALIVE.

In a 1992 interview with Parade, Wanyá spoke about how Khalil's wisdom and perspective on life informed Boyz II Men's approach to live performances. "The message we're trying to get across to people is that they should spread love," he said. "Khalil explained to us that, onstage, you can have hurt and anger inside you, but it can't be shown to the people. They want to see your best performance, and if the hurt and anger they feel can be taken away by your performance, you'll feel better."

Khalil would not be the only Rountree to pursue a life in entertainment. Today, Rountree's son, Khalil Rountree Jr., is a celebrated MMA fighter. In a 2024 interview for ESPN's UFC 307 Countdown, Rountree Jr. spoke about his father's funeral and the outpouring of support offered by the community in the wake of his death. "At his funeral, I remember there being hundreds, if not thousands, of people," he remembered. "When I think about that, you've got to be a certain type of person to have complete strangers and just a massive amount of people coming to your funeral to honor your life."

▶ The group poses with Khalil Rountree in 1989.

CHAPTER 6

A JOYOUS SOUND

OVERCOMING OBSTACLES AND BREAKING BARRIERS

BOYZ II MEN PERFORMED ON THE POPULAR British television show *Top of the Pops* the same week that "End Of The Road" broke Elvis's record for consecutive weeks at No. 1 on the *Billboard* charts. The popular BBC program had been running weekly since 1964 and featured the top-charting musical acts from around the world. Throughout its history, *Top of the Pops* has featured a who's who of important British acts of the last sixty years, from the Rolling Stones, David Bowie, to Kate Bush to New Order and Culture Club, and on through to 808 State and Oasis. The evolution of pop music in the late twentieth and early twenty-first centuries can be traced through *Top of the Pops* performances.

◄ Boyz II Men at the Soul Train Music Awards in 1992.

► The stage for BBC program *Top of the Pops*, circa 1970.

On November 12, 1992, Boyz II Men brought their smash hit to the BBC studios. This wasn't the first time Boyz II Men had sung "End Of The Road" on *Top of the Pops*. It was customary for charting acts to perform the same popular song multiple times on the show, so the group had also performed the song in October and September of that year. Another *Top of the Pops* custom was to have artists lip sync to a recording of their hit song, similar to its American counterpart, *Soul Train*. The exact reasons why this was done

remain the thing of rumor and speculation, but by the 1990s, the producers had relaxed the lip sync rule, allowing artists to sing live over a backing track.

For Boyz II Men, any opportunity to sing live and showcase their vocal prowess was a win, and the November 12 performance was a revelation. Recorded in the midst of a lengthy tour, the Boyz's voices sounded strained, and the performance was much rawer than what anyone had grown used to hearing from the group, a far cry from the polished, well-crafted singing heard on the recorded version. The energy of the song's sweeping, defiant chorus was far more subdued. But the imperfections of the live performance both highlighted the vulnerability and sadness of the song and showed that the group was able to deliver a performance that was technically imprecise yet still emotionally moving. The members of Boyz II Men were tired, overworked, and grinding it out over 3,500 miles away from their hometown, but the *Top of the Pops* performances were viewed by millions in England, signaling to the important market that Boyz II Men were legit, doing the work, and ready for whatever the music business threw at them next.

Despite the outsized influence that Black American music has had on the world, true mainstream pop stardom has historically been an elusive status for Black artists. No matter how many records they sell or who they sell them to, most are still perceived differently than their white counterparts. It is much more difficult for a successful Black artist to transcend their given genre and achieve the universal broad appeal of a mainstream pop star, likely due to the fact that genre itself has always been directly tied to race. In the 1920s, when the record and radio industries were in their infancy, the practice of categorizing and marketing Black musical styles and artists by race was common. So common was this practice that the Okeh Label produced a series of blues, jazz, and spiritual music that Okeh staff producer Ralph S. Peer dubbed "race records." To market these records to Black audiences and likely to assure potential buyers that the artist on the record was indeed Black, Okeh would include portraits of their artists in advertisements printed in prominent Black newspapers around the country.

> *Despite the outsized influence that Black American music has had on the world, true mainstream pop stardom has historically been an elusive status for Black artists.*

Eventually, the term "race records" or "race music" would give way to "rhythm & blues," but race remained forever baked into perceptions of musical genres. R&B, rock, and hip-hop acts must transcend genre constraints and grow beyond their core audiences to even have a chance at ascending to the level of pop stardom. In the mainstream music industry, pop rests at the top of a commercial hierarchy, and it is a hierarchy in which race (and class) are key determinants. Black musicians are rarely afforded entry into the broad, race-neutral universality of pop stardom.

A good pop-culture example of this appears in Spike Lee's classic 1989 film, *Do the Right Thing*. A character named Mookie (played by Lee) confronts his coworker, Pino, a white man and flagrant racist who happens to admire the work of Black mainstream pop cultural figures. After Pino goes on a racist tirade, Mookie asks him a series of questions to point out the hypocrisy of his racist attitudes. Pino says that Magic Johnson is his favorite basketball player and Eddie Murphy is his favorite movie star, and, though Pino denies it, Mookie points out that Prince is his favorite rock star. Mookie then asks Pino how he can hate Black people so much when all his "favorite people" are Black. Flustered by these clear contradictions, Pino stutters out a half-formed response, trying to explain to Mookie that these beloved pop culture icons are "Black, but they're not *really* Black. They're more than Black."

Within this fictional exchange lies an important insight into how Black stars in America are often perceived by white audiences. Black artists are held in a racialized box within the American popular consciousness, denied the kind of all-encompassing, mainstream fame that white artists achieve, and when they do get big enough or prestigious enough to reach that higher stratum, in the minds of some, they cease to be Black at all.

All these racial, social, and historical dynamics remain today as part of the fabric of American popular culture. In 1993, "End Of The Road" had enjoyed a record-breaking run on the *Billboard* charts, and it seemed as though Boyz II Men had become both inescapable and undeniable.

On January 19, 1993, the day before Bill Clinton was sworn into office, Boyz II Men took part in the Presidential Inaugural Celebration for Youth. This star-studded concert aired on the Disney Channel and was hosted by fellow Philadelphian Will Smith. President-elect Clinton and his wife Hilary made appearances alongside performances by Celine Dion, Vanessa Williams, Kenny Loggins, and the Los Angeles Youth Ensemble Theater. Boyz II Men were asked to perform twice during the broadcast, a testament to their popularity and mainstream appeal.

Following a short round of onstage banter between Smith and Clinton, the group came out fast and furious with an energetic rendition of "Motownphilly." Rocking matching turtleneck pullovers and sweaters, the group's preppy look was in full effect, and they didn't hold back at all in bringing energy to the stage. After coaxing the crowd to participate and wave their hands in the air, the band launched into a choreographed routine that was part Temptations, part New Edition, reflecting two of the group's core influences. Nate's part of the first verse

▼ Boyz II Men at the 20th Annual American Music Awards, 1993. The group won the award for Favorite Soul/R&B Duo or Group.

was smooth and understated, while Wanyá's part came in like a bolt of lightning, lifting the energy back and sending the crowd sailing into the chorus. The racially mixed, mostly pre-teen and adolescent crowd screamed throughout the song, and kids crowded around the foot of the stage to get a closer look at the group.

In the winter of 1993, there were no other male R&B groups so deeply rooted in Black music culture who would've had this kind of effect on this audience. In fact, most of Boyz II Men's peers would never have been invited to a youth event coordinated by the president-elect's Inauguration Committee or Disney in the first place. This has nothing to do with the quality of music that contemporaneous male R&B groups were making at the time. Boyz II Men conquering the pop landscape happened because of a combination of music and marketing.

The band's youth and the clean-cut image that Bivins helped them cultivate played a huge role in how the band was marketed in those early years. In a December 2006 profile for *Vibe*, writer-turned-filmmaker Laura Checkoway spoke with the group about their image and their initial reservations about how they were being presented to the public. "BIIM's clean-cut image was a refreshing shift from the bump-'n'-grind R&B that ruled the early 1990s, but the group had its misgivings," Checkoway wrote. Wanyá said, "We were a little apprehensive about walking the streets in Philly with that preppy Alex Vanderpool Biv on, but we had to live it."

Toward the end of the pre-inauguration show, Boyz II Men returned to the stage to sing a harmonically rich, a cappella verse of "The Star-Spangled Banner." Dressed in matching blue suit jackets, the quartet poured into this gorgeous, complex take on America's anthem. The four guys from the poor and working-class neighborhoods of Philly had transformed themselves into a clean-cut quartet with a smooth, digestible sound.

U KNOW

"By the time 'End Of The Road' came out, a lot of people had mad respect for Boyz II Men because they were good. I mean . . . they weren't just good, they were great. They had great voices and production and we hadn't heard music like that in a long time."
—*Michael Gonzales, music journalist*

Six days later, on January 25, 1993, the 20th Annual American Music Awards were held at the Shrine Auditorium, in Los Angeles, California. The show was hosted by Latin pop sensation Gloria Estefan, country music star Wynonna Judd, and New Edition alumnus Bobby Brown. That night, Boyz II Men were nominated for awards in two categories. These nominations not only reflected the group's popularity, but also showed how that popularity shaped industry perceptions of the group. Predictably, Boyz II Men were nominated for Favorite Soul/R&B Band/Duo/Group, with Jodeci and the Oakland-based group En Vogue as stiff competition. "End Of The Road" was also nominated for Favorite Pop/Rock Single, a nomination that spoke to the song's dominance and the group's crossover appeal.

The award for Favorite Soul/R&B Band Duo or Group was presented by reggae artists Shabba Ranks and Mad Cobra, and the Queen of Hip-Hop Soul, Mary J. Blige, and when the time came, Boyz II Men were the victors. The band accepted their award and huddled close together around the podium while Wanyá repeatedly exclaimed, "Thank you, Jesus!" overwhelmed with the emotional weight of the moment. Nate, acting as the group's spokesman offered a solemn dedication to the mentor and friend they'd lost eight months prior: "This one is for the man that has given us everything that we have and his

family. His name is Mr. Khalil Rountree. We love you. Thank you."

> "This one is for the man that has given us everything that we have and his family. His name is Mr. Khalil Rountree. We love you. Thank you."

For Favorite Pop/Rock Single, the group faced off against two juggernauts: Mariah Carey and Trey Lorenz's cover of the Jackson 5's "I'll Be There" and Red Hot Chili Pepper's "Under The Bridge." Boyz II Men and "End Of The Road" triumphed again, a win that further cemented the song's status as a crossover hit. During the post-win interview, Nate fought through a stream of tears to further express the band's debt and gratitude to Khalil Rountree. "Everything that you see us do from day to day . . . everything was taught to us by him and we felt him here with us tonight."

The group returned to the Shrine a month later for the 35th Annual Grammy Awards. The awards show took place just four years after the 1989 Grammy ceremony which was famously boycotted by a group of young hip-hop artists who were nominated that year. Artists like Will Smith and his partner DJ

▲ Boyz II Men at the 35th
Annual Grammy Awards.

Jazzy Jeff, Salt-N-Pepa, and LL Cool J chose not to attend because of the Grammy producers' choice not to air the presentation for Best Rap Performance on television. In a 1989 interview with *Entertainment Tonight*, Smith and Jazzy Jeff aired their grievances with the Grammys and explained how they felt disrespected by the famed institution.

"We chose to boycott. We feel that it's a slap in the face," Smith said.

"They said there wasn't enough time to televise all of the categories," Jeff recalled. "They televised sixteen categories and, from record sales, from the *Billboard* charts, from the overall public's view, there's no way you can tell me that out of sixteen categories, that rap isn't in the top sixteen."

The nominees for Best Rap Performance that year were stacked with future classics. Kool Moe Dee—who went against the boycott and replaced Smith as a presenter—got a nod for his "Wild Wild West" single. J.J. Fad's "Supersonic," LL Cool J's "Going Back To Cali," Salt-N-Pepa's "Push It," and DJ Jazzy Jeff and the Fresh Prince's "Parents Just Don't Understand" rounded out the list of nominees. "Parents Just Don't Understand" ended up winning Best Rap Performance that night, but that moment in history would be forever tainted. It was the first year that a Grammy Award had been given out for rap music and the group that won wasn't there to accept it.

In 1993, rap music was well represented at the Grammys, with Arrested Development's win for Best New Artist, Sir Mix-A-Lot's Best Rap Solo Performance win, and nominees like MC Hammer, LL Cool J, Public Enemy, the Beastie Boys, and more. In addition to the traditional rap acts that received acknowledgment from the academy, hip-hop-informed R&B acts like Bobby Brown, TLC, and Boyz II Men were also nominated.

> *Nate, Shawn, Michael, and Wanyá left the Shrine with more trophies than Michael Jackson, a secure place atop R&B's fiercely competitive hierarchy, and a clear pathway to pop stardom.*

Fresh off a sweep at the American Music Awards, Boyz II Men and "End Of The Road" were favorites to win at least one Grammy that night. In addition to performing and presenting the award for Best Female Pop Vocal Performance alongside Philly vocal powerhouse Patti LaBelle, Boyz II Men also won an award for Best R&B Performance by a Duo or Group with Vocal for "End Of The Road." The song's writers, Daryl Simmons, Babyface, and L.A. Reid, were also nominated

► From left to right, Patti LaBelle, Luther Vandross, and Natalie Cole, hosts of the 7th Annual Soul Train Awards, 1993.

for Best Rhythm & Blues Song—and won. By racking up two Grammy wins that night while continuing to make a strong showing on the charts, "End Of The Road" solidified itself as the song of the year.

March 9, 1993, brought another award show and another round of victories for the group. The Soul Train Music Awards were also held at the Shrine Auditorium, but this time, the venue was packed with Black music legends performing and presenting for a majority Black audience. Patti LaBelle, Natalie Cole, and Luther Vandross opened the ceremony and the King of Pop himself, Michael Jackson, even performed his colossal hit "Remember The Time" in a wheelchair, having hurt his ankle during rehearsal the night before. The Soul Train Music Awards would find Nate, Shawn, Wanyá, and Michael taking a victory lap of sorts. After two years of navigating the delicate dance of crossing over and cleaning up at the Grammys and the American Music Awards, Boyz II Men now found themselves with the biggest pop hit of their young career. It was time for Boyz II Men to receive their flowers from their fellow Black musicians and industry professionals.

For their Soul Train Awards performance, Boyz II Men performed a medley of songs, beginning with a subdued, a cappella version of "Please Don't Go" before the backing band kicked into gear, playing a nimble, tempo-pushing take on "Motownphilly." The group launched into a high-powered Temptations-meets-Hammer-style dance routine, a far cry from their skills—or lack thereof—in 1989, when Michael Bivins had lamented the group's poor dancing skills. After a brief detour into "Uhh Ahh," they delivered the main course with a rousing version of "End Of The Road." That six-minute medley was a primer on Boyz II Men, from their a cappella skills to the dance moves to their sex appeal. The crowd in the auditorium clapped and cheered as Wanyá's powerful, churchy runs lit up the Shrine.

"End Of The Road" won Song Of The Year and Best Music Video that night. In a less obvious choice, "Please Don't Go" won Best R&B/Soul Single – Group, Band, or Duo. The award was presented by Jamie Foxx, Toni Braxton, and Chris "Daddy Mac" Smith of Kris Kross, and winning it represented a subtle nod of approval from the Black music community. The group beat out Arrested Development, Vanessa Williams, and En Vogue. Much like the Grammys and the American Music Awards, that night was a sweep for Boyz II Men, winning every award they were nominated for. Nate, Shawn, Michael, and Wanyá left the Shrine with more trophies than Michael Jackson, a secure place atop R&B's fiercely competitive hierarchy, and a clear pathway to pop stardom.

RACE, MUSIC, AND CROSSING OVER

LIKE ANY CULTURAL PHENOMENON BORN IN AND SHAPED BY THE UNITED STATES, THE HISTORY OF AMERICAN POPULAR MUSIC IS INEXTRICABLY TIED TO RACE AND RACISM. THE EMERGENCE OF THE RECORD INDUSTRY NOT ONLY DOVETAILED WITH THE BIRTH OF SECULAR BLACK MUSICAL STYLES LIKE THE BLUES AND JAZZ. ALL THE TECHNOLOGICAL, INDUSTRIAL. AND CULTURAL INNOVATIONS HAPPENED AGAINST THE BACKDROP OF JIM CROW.

Following Thomas Edison's invention of the phonograph in 1877, a number of ambitious record companies were founded with the hopes of capitalizing on the demand for recorded music. Upon identifying a profitable market for Black music, record companies like Okeh, Columbia, and Paramount began producing Black music records that they marketed as "race records."

In a 2016 interview with Washington Post Live, author and music journalist Danyel Smith spoke about how race records and segregation defined the popular music charts along racial lines. "I used to work at *Billboard* . . . There are the R&B charts and there are the pop charts and essentially that's shorthand for really the Black charts and the white mainstream charts. So the idea of 'crossing over' meant that you crossed over from what actually used to be called the 'race charts,' the 'negro charts,' and in unkind circles, the 'N-word charts.' So, people would strive to cross over to the pop charts. That meant they were selling more records, that meant that they could play larger and more beautiful venues and sell tickets for more. Their music could be played on radio stations that were marketed to white and mainstream audiences."

As the Blues and Black spiritual music of the 1920s, 1930s, and 1940s evolved into rock 'n' roll, the term "race records" fell out of favor, but the practice of categorizing and marketing music along segregated racial lines remained. By the 1950s, popular Black rock artists like Little Richard, Chuck Berry, and Bo Diddley enjoyed broad mainstream appeal, attracting large white audiences. Despite these artist's success and the general popularity of rock 'n' roll, Black musicians still had to make humiliating concessions to segregation, like entering into venues through the kitchen and performing segregated events with a rope dividing Black and white attendees across the dance floor. Any cultural unity that pop music may have engendered between Black and white audiences was in constant danger of cracking under the weight of racial apartheid/Jim Crow.

While record companies marketed rock music and Black artists to white youth, a nationwide backlash sprung up as white Christian groups and parental associations protested the music on the grounds of its imagined capacity to "corrupt" white teenage music fans. While much of the anti-rock rhetoric was shrouded in religious terms and claims that rock 'n' roll was "the devil's music," it is clear that the moral panic around rock also had racial motivations.

In a 2017 address titled "Rock 'n' roll and 'moral panics' - Part One: 1950s and 1960s," an associate professor of sociology at the University of Southern Indiana named Steve Williams spoke to rock 'n' roll's Black origins and how the music's association with Black people led to white fears of sexual relations between Black men and white women.

"Rock 'n' roll is not just an American invention, but it's an African American invention," Williams said. "If you look at basic rock 'n' roll, the fundamental formula is basically African American blues with a little more speed and electricity. One of the moral panics associated with the first wave of rock 'n' roll was the fear of race mixing—that young Black and white kids would get together over this music that had a rhythmic, primitive, sensuous

beat. Suburban moms and dads are freaked out about their daughters hanging out with young Black men listening to sexualized music."

On the other side of the color line, Black people had a completely different response to the racial divide in American music and popular culture. In a 2021 talk with the Arvada Center titled "Race & The Myth of Rock 'n' Roll," Dr. Shana L. Redmon explained how Black activists understood that segregation in culture reinforced social and political segregation and fought against it.

"I think that . . . all of these [media] industries were playing an active role in the maintenance of Jim Crow segregation," Dr. Redmon said. "They saw it as their mission, so much so that you have the National Association for the Advancement of Colored People developing an entire kind of task force in response to popular culture and trying to break down those boundaries by lobbying Hollywood, lobbying the FCC by doing all of these things to say you actually can't hold this line anymore. The streets are marching and they're telling you that Jim Crow must die, and you have to reflect that in popular culture."

Racial stratification was built into the bones of American popular music. Our conception of genre and mainstream accessibility are all undergirded by race. Black musicians, in particular, have had to engage in the delicate dance of the crossover, maintaining their musical and cultural authenticity while appealing to larger white audiences conditioned to hate them. Whether one considers rock 'n' roll in the 1950s, Motown in the 1960s, the disco explosion of the 1970s, the rise of Black pop stars like Michael Jackson and Prince or hip-hop's takeover of the mainstream in the 1980 and 1990s, the story of American pop music is the story of how Black musicians have navigated the country's racist composition.

CHAPTER 7

II

THE BAND'S SOPHOMORE ALBUM

N OCTOBER OF 1993, BOYZ II MEN released *Christmas Interpretations*, an album of Christmas-themed songs. The project debuted at No.1 on the *Billboard* Top R&B Albums charts and a 2022 retrospective piece by *Counterpunch* hailed the album as "the best, most complete, Christmas album of the modern era." With the exception of *Christmas Interpretations*, the winning year of 1993 did not bring the release of any new music from Boyz II Men.

◄ Boyz II Men in 1993.

Bolstered by the runaway success of "End Of The Road," the group became fixtures in the pop cultural landscape. In addition to the pre-inauguration performance and award shows, the band made appearances on both late-night and early-morning television talk shows. On November 23, the group made an appearance on the wildly popular Arsenio Hall Show to promote *Christmas Interpretations*. In between a brief interview segment, the group performed "You Are Not Alone" and "Let It Snow" with the song's cowriter, Brian McKnight. In December 1993, Boyz II Men even popped up on The Fresh Prince of Bel Air, in a Christmas episode in which Will lies to his family, claiming that he booked Boyz II Men to sing at his nephew's christening. Hijinks ensue, and the band appears in the nick of time—in church, no less—to perform a dreamy, ethereal version of "Silent Night."

When *Cooleyhighharmony* was released in 1991, Boyz II Men were big. Throughout 1992 and 1993, they were inescapable, with palpable anticipation for their next album. While the next Boyz II Men album would bring new creative opportunities for the group, the recording process had its share of friction and difficulty. At its core, *Cooleyhighharmony* was the product of a single musical partnership between the group and the album's producer, Dallas Austin. Charles Farrar and Troy Taylor

are credited for their work on the album's two closing songs, "Little Things" and "Your Love," but the bulk of the album was done by Austin. When it came time to record a proper follow-up, Austin refused, later citing personal conflicts with the group and a distaste for their post-fame attitudes. Although Austin reluctantly agreed to work on one track for the album that would become *II*, Boyz II Men would no longer have him to rely on.

It was around 1993 when complications from Michael's then-undiagnosed multiple sclerosis began to intensify. In 2016, Michael spoke about his health issues on author and inspirational speaker Iyanla Vanzant's reality show, *Iyanla, Fix My Life*. "I was in Boyz II Men, I first saw some of the ailments start to happen," he shared. "It was like little back spasms at first. And then they would get stronger and stronger, so each time it would get more harsh. Once I was about twenty-two, it started going to full scale. They were saying that I have a nerve around the sciatica that was locked in place that could sever if I stepped wrong. I could be paralyzed."

The band soldiered on, and the dissolution of their partnership with Austin (their primary producer), the passage of time, and changing tastes naturally resulted in a noticeable change in the group's sound. The frenetic, New Jack Swing-influenced beats that Austin was producing in the late 1990s were replaced by songs with a more relaxed approached to fusing hip-hop and R&B. The ballads still featured meticulously arranged instrumentation and vocal harmonies, but they were sonically closer to "End Of The Road" than earlier songs like "Please Don't Go," which still had a bit of the polish of 1980s/early 1990s R&B. In addition to these changes in personnel and style, *II* differed from *Cooleyhighharmony* in the sheer amount of time it took to create. Since their debut, the band had toured the world and built entirely new lives for themselves. While the first album was recorded in about six weeks, the second took about nine months, with the band reportedly recording thirty songs before paring down to the thirteen that appear on the final album.

The album opens with the sole Dallas Austin-produced track, "Thank You." Built around beatboxed vocal percussion and doo-wop-style harmonies, the song is a clever flip on the a cappella concept, as the backing track is essentially a hip-hop beat composed entirely of human voices. With a nod to the street corner doo-wop of the past and the beatbox rhythm of the present, Boyz II Men reinforce an integral part of their identity as a group: a bridge between generations and stylings. They are contemporary practitioners of doo-wop and inheritors of hip-hop.

As an opener, "Thank You" is perfect. While the lyrics express gratitude to unnamed loved ones who've supported the members throughout tough times, it wouldn't be hard to imagine millions of Boyz II Men fans pressing play on the album in 1994 and feeling like they were being thanked themselves. The next track, "All Around The World," is the first of two songs produced by legendary production team Jimmy Jam and Terry Lewis. Motown CEO Jheryl Busby, overseeing the project as executive producer, connected the band with the veteran producers, hoping to take advantage of the duo's experience and track record of producing hit songs.

By the time they got to work on *II*, Jam and Lewis had already established themselves as one of the greatest songwriting and production teams in popular music. Emerging from Minneapolis' impossibly rich funk and R&B scene, Jimmy Jam and Terry Lewis inevitably hooked up with another star of the scene, Prince Rogers Nelson. With ambitions and music to spare, Prince recruited Jam and Lewis to join the side band he had created, the Time. Unfortunately, Jam and Lewis were unceremoniously fired after a snowstorm caused them to miss a Time gig while they were moonlighting at a session for the S.O.S. Band. Free of Prince's controlling hand, Jam and Lewis went on to dominate the 1980s

◄ Boyz II Men's appearance on a Christmas special episode of *The Fresh Prince of Bel Air.*

► Boyz II
Men in Munich,
Germany, 1994.

and 1990s, producing a number of hits for Janet Jackson, Cheryl Lynn, Patti LaBelle, Cherrelle, Alexander O'Neal—and Boyz II Men.

II's "All Around The World" finds the Boyz taking account of life on the road and how the preceding three years had changed their lives. Anchored by a bouncy, hip-hop backbeat, the song's lyrics are direct and self-referential, with the group inviting listeners to join them on another journey "back around the world" and listing the names of women they met on their journeys.

Once we get to "U Know," there's a noticeable difference in how *II* is sequenced when compared to *Cooleyhighharmony*. Whereas the first album's A-side was heavy with ballads, the second album places the up-tempo, hip-hop-influenced songs up front. The first few bars of "U Know" have an ominous feel, with sampled guitars and synth pad, and once the beat fully kicks in, it's heavy and unrelenting. The drums are the centerpiece here, taken from the Five Stairsteps' "Don't Change Your Love," a heavily sampled tune from 1968 written and produced by Curtis Mayfield. While "U Know" is not a slow song, it is a thematic return to the kind of deep romantic pain and yearning at the heart of some of Boyz II Men's greatest ballads.

The following song, "Vibin'," is a breezy, laid-back tune about the joy of music creation, with the group singing over a slick instrumental with a syncopated synth bass similar to the lines that producer and New Jack Swing inventor Teddy Riley would play on records. Shawn opens the first verse, bringing us into the studio at the moment of creation; everything is peaceful, everyone is free to make music until the sun comes up. Nate's second verse transports the listener to a dark basement party that could be in Philly or any other city worldwide. Drinks are flowing, men and women dance together, and the DJ controls the music. The chorus on "Vibin'" is simple lyrically, but stacked with dense, complex harmonies perfect for this loving tribute to the joy of music.

Tucked at the end of *II*'s first side and never released as a single, "I Sit Away" is a sleeper in Boyz II Men's catalog, but significant nonetheless. A gorgeous and soulful meditation on loneliness, the song was penned and produced by Detroit-born singer-songwriter Tony Rich, a standout with sorrowful, poetic lyrics backed by Rich's atmospheric production full of keys, acoustic guitar, and electric bass. The group reflects on the feeling of being isolated and longing for connection, a seemingly ironic idea coming from four young men at the height of their fame. But the choice to include "I Sit

◄ Jimmy Jam
and Terry Lewis,
producers of *II* (1994).

Away" on *II* hints that they were longing for connections that their status couldn't provide. In their 1995 fan photobook *Us II You,* Shawn spoke about how the band's early success caught the members off guard, leaving him longing for certain aspects of a regular life. "Sometimes I think too much has happened to us too fast," he said at the time. "Things are moving too fast to enjoy the simple things, like a kiss from a girl that loves you. I'm not able to experience that, to experience those small things that mean something to a person."

> *"Sometimes I think too much has happened to us too fast. Things are moving too fast to enjoy the simple things."*

"Jezzebel" is the Side A's closer and the song's stacked, jazz-influenced vocal harmonies reveal the depths of Take 6's influence on Boyz II Men. Telling a story of the members trying to bag an attractive young lady on the train, the lyrics find the band showing off a playfully seductive side. What's most interesting about "Jezzebel" is the musical arrangement. The jazz influences are evident in the piano chords and swinging bassline. The group complements the jazz influence by adding elements of vocal scatting to their delivery.

The second half of the album opens with "Khalil (Interlude)," a gorgeous musical tribute to the memory of Khalil Rountree. Backed by a somber piano, the group mourn the loss of Rountree and reflect on his role as a mentor and protector. Perhaps due to the real-life tragedy that inspired the song, "Khalil (Interlude)" remains one of the most poignant songs that Boyz II Men have ever created. In a 2019 interview published to celebrate the twenty-fifth anniversary of *II,* the group spoke with *Billboard* about the song. "It was Michael Bivins' idea to do a tribute song for Khalil," Wanyá said. "We were all talking about it and he was like, 'Y'all should do it.' Next thing you know, we just came up with that in the studio playing the piano. It was one of those things that organically happened."

"That was still a tough time for us because it was the first album we did where he wasn't around," Nate added. "That kind of helped us get through it, knowing what he would've wanted us to do. Being able to come up with something like that to honor him and his family and let people know how much he meant to us. The transition we were taking that time from boys to men by ourselves was a lot."

Much like the position that "Please Don't Go" occupied on *Cooleyhighharmony,* "Khalil (Interlude)" set the tone for a full side of heartfelt ballads. Musically and thematically, "Trying Times" wears the influence of New Edition's "Can You Stand The Rain" on its sleeve. With the duo of Tim & Bob (Tim Kelley and Bob Robinson) laying down a silky piano-led instrumental, Michael opens with a monologue about reconciliation. While pledging his undying love, he hopes that both he and his partner can find the strength to weather the unnamed strife that has been challenging their relationship. Robinson's jazz piano adds a distinct element to the song, and the tune closes with a gorgeous group harmony section that sets up two of the group's biggest and most enduring hit songs.

"I'll Make Love To You" and "On Bended Knee" are not only the highlights of *II*, both songs have become defining moments for Boyz II Men. It's not often that a group has four songs that could make the case for a signature song, but in 1994, "I'll Make Love To You" and "On Bended Knee" joined "Motownphilly" and "End Of The Road" as smash hits and career-defining compositions for the group. The influence of both songs on the group's career and R&B music as a whole were

► Boyz II Men attend MTV's Fourth Annual Rock N' Jock B-Ball Jam in September 1994.

significant and deserving of a more in-depth exploration; more on the creation and impact of these masterful ballads in the next chapter.

Following "On Bended Knee" on *II*'s track list is fan favorite "50 Candles." Steeped in velvety romanticism, "50 Candles" is a seductive song centered around a deep upright bassline and the group's impeccable harmonizing. Nate and Shawn take first verse duties, ready to lose themselves in the act of making love. The chorus introduces a dreamlike harmony, and the song takes on a hazy atmosphere unlike anything else on *II*. "50 Candles" is the closest sonically to *Cooleyhighharmony*. It's not necessarily a step back musically, but the sound is reminiscent of the late 1980s and early 1990s ballad style the group mined on the first album. For live renditions of the song, the group's production team would light fifty candles lined up along the front of the stage.

Beyond the two smash singles "I'll Make Love To You" and "On Bended Knee," "Water Runs Dry"—an elegant, bittersweet ballad written and produced by Babyface—might be the standout song on Boyz II Men's second album. After the unprecedented success of "End Of The Road," Motown naturally wanted the group to work with Babyface again. And "Water Runs Dry" was like nothing else in the group's catalog. From the distinct vocal phrasing on the verses to the acoustic guitar sound, everything about the song bore Babyface's signature. Rhythmically, the pacing of "Water Runs Dry" is held by a march-like kick and snare pattern, a solemn atmosphere reinforced by Babyface's heart-wrenching lyrics. The first verse paints a picture of a couple amid a full communication breakdown. Despite all of their pain and strife, Babyface's lyrics still call for healing and reconciliation. For the chorus, the couple's loss of warmth and intimacy is cast as a metaphorical "water," nourishment that keeps the relationship alive. Babyface pleads with his love that they not let the water run dry. The bridge offers a moment of hope, but it is immediately undercut by the admission that some embattled lovers just don't know how to change. It's a strikingly mature and sober take on love and relationships, brought to life by Boyz II Men's stellar voices.

II closes with a cover of "Yesterday" by the Beatles. A deeply sad breakup song written by Paul McCartney, "Yesterday" was originally released in 1965 and has since become a standard. It is rightfully regarded as a high point in the Beatles' storied catalog. Boyz II Men may have chosen to close their album with this song for a variety of reasons. With the crossover success of "End Of The Road," the group could've anticipated that an influx of new fans would be checking out *II*. Many of these fans would've been white pop and rock fans and "Yesterday" was a slam dunk if Boyz II Men wanted to offer these new fans a cover of a familiar song. Many of the Beatles' formative influences were also Black rockers like Little Richard and Chuck Berry, with Motown influencing them later, so perhaps Boyz II Men wanted to keep that cycle going. There could also have been a musical incentive for covering "Yesterday." For all its emotional and lyrical complexity, McCartney's song is deceptively minimal and simple, allowing Nate, Shawn, Wanyá, and Michael to experiment. In Boyz II Men's hands, McCartney's lead vocal melody is morphed and augmented with complex harmonies.

The band's cover offers a fresh take on the classic composition, but it was not the only time the Beatles' music has been reimagined by Black artists. With her brilliant versions of "Hey Jude" and "Eleanor Rigby," Aretha Franklin was one of the great interpreters of the Beatles' music, while soul legends like Tina Turner, Otis Redding, Stevie Wonder, and James Brown have all taken a swing at covering the Fab Four's music. Of course, there was a clear economic incentive for Black artists to perform these covers. Much like every facet of American society in the 1960s and 1970s, the music industry was deeply segregated. For many Black artists, the pathway to a wider audience outside their core Black demographic was to cover the music of popular white artists. In the hands of Black soul, funk, and jazz musicians, these songs took on new dimensions and another life.

In a 2024 interview with *People*, Shawn reflects on "Yesterday" and Paul McCartney's reaction to the Boyz II Men version. "We did get a letter from him. He said he and his late wife, Linda, were just coming from dinner. I can hear him saying, 'We're going to dinner. And we hopped in the car, and we turned on the radio, and we heard your beautiful rendition. We just had to say it was one of the most beautiful renditions of a song that we have ever written, and we'd like to thank you.'"

Whether its inclusion was a choice made for commercial or musical reasons or both, Boyz II Men's version of "Yesterday" fittingly closes out the second side of their second album. McCartney's lyrics and melody have an air of regret to them, giving the song a palpable feeling of finality. There's a longing feeling that permeates many of the ballads on *II*, signaling that along with the maturity of age, the group had unlocked a new degree of vulnerability in their music. A pair of songs from *II* put the heartfelt vulnerability on full display, a pair of magnum opuses that would dominate 1994 and go down as two of the most beloved songs of all time.

A BEHIND-THE-SCENES INTERVIEW WITH . . .

REGGIE HAMILTON IS A VETERAN ELECTRIC AND UPRIGHT BASS-IST. HAVING WORKED WITH EVERYONE FROM TINA TURNER AND TONI BRAXTON TO BETTE MIDLER, WHITNEY HOUSTON, AND MARIAH CAREY, HAMILTON IS ONE OF THE MOST IN-DEMAND SESSION MUSICIANS IN THE INDUSTRY. A FREQUENT COLLAB-ORATOR WITH KENNETH "BABYFACE" EDMONDS, HAMILTON PLAYED ON CLASSIC BOYZ II MEN/BABYFACE HITS "I'LL MAKE LOVE TO YOU" AND "WATER RUNS DRY."

▶ **CAN YOU TELL ME A LITTLE BIT ABOUT YOUR BACKGROUND? HOW'D YOU GET INTO MUSIC?**

I started as a child. My mom bought me a guitar when I was five and I started taking lessons at seven. I switched to bass at eleven and a friend of mine, this guy named Chris Martin, who was part of the group Kid 'n Play, he got me into my first band.

▶ **OH, WOW. WHAT BAND WAS IT?**

It was a little band that we had called Blue Velvet, a little R&B group. We played an Apollo talent show one night. We only brought our mothers to come and applaud us and we still did really well.

▶ **WERE Y'ALL PLAYING COVERS OR ORIGINALS?**

We were playing covers in the beginning, like Earth, Wind & Fire, the Commodores, P-Funk, just whatever was popular. We're talking about '75, '76?

▶ **HOW DID YOU MAKE THAT TRANSITION FROM PLAYING IN A SMALL BAND TO ACTUALLY BEING IN THE RECORD BUSINESS?**

Oh, the record business. It really didn't hit for me until I moved to Los Angeles. A friend of mine, guy named Mike Pedicin, this great saxophone player who used to be in this group called MFSB, he was my boss in Atlantic City. I worked for him and he made me move to LA. I played on one of his records and then right after that, I sold everything I didn't need, threw the rest in my car, and drove to LA.

▶ **WHAT WAS THE LOGIC BEHIND THE MOVE? WAS IT LIKE "HEY, YOU CAN COME OUT TO LA, DO SOME SESSIONS AND GET MORE GIGS," THAT SORT OF THING?**

No, no. His logic was "You're gonna die in Atlantic City." I was gonna crash my car, or some girl's gonna kill me, or I'm gonna drink or do some drugs, or something like that.

▶ **WOW. LIVING THE FAST LIFE.**

I was young, man. I was twenty years old with money in my pocket. So, I could either go back to New York, Paris, or go to LA. There's nothing worse than having an upright bass in the middle of a winter storm on the subway or living in Queens and having to drive to the city for a $50 gig. None of that sounded appealing. And Paris . . . I spoke a little French, not a lot. So I'd have been an outsider. LA was warm, I knew some people. So, I drove out, rented a room from my ex-girlfriend for about a month. My first year, I met [bassist/composer] Stanley Clarke; the year after, I met [jazz pianist] Billy Childs. Through Stanley, I met [drummer] Rayford Griffin, and Rayford introduced me to Babyface. That's how I got to do the Boyz II Men stuff.

▶ **WHAT DO YOU REMEMBER ABOUT THE "I'LL MAKE LOVE TO YOU" SESSION?**

Well, for me, it was pretty simple, because whenever I worked with Kenny [Babyface], if he didn't have a melody, I'd ask him to sing the melody at least one time. Rayford programmed the drums. It was a nice groove and then I recorded the bass. I think it took me fifteen minutes.

▶ **"END OF THE ROAD" WAS SUPER HUGE. DID YOU HAVE ANY SENSE THAT "I'LL MAKE LOVE TO YOU" WOULD BE THIS MASSIVE HIT?**

No, no. Not a clue. I had no idea until a friend of mine who worked at Motown told me that they had shipped double platinum. Which is crazy.

▶ **THEY WERE EXPECTING IT TO SELL LIKE HOTCAKES.**

Yeah. But I don't think that they expected it to sell that many, like twenty million copies.

▲ Reggie Hamilton performs in 2021.

WHAT'S NEXT?

THE RISE OF "I'LL MAKE LOVE TO YOU" AND "ON BENDED KNEE"

N THE MUSIC BUSINESS, A HIT RECORD can be both a gift and a curse. The money, success, accolades, and praise can be life-changing for an artist at any stage of their career, but especially in those crucial early stages. The annals of music history are filled with uplifting, feel-good stories of artists who wrote a song that hit it big by chance. The doors that a hit record will open and the opportunities that it can facilitate can positively change an artist's life in immeasurable ways. However, a hit record can also be an albatross.

◀ Boyz II Men attend the 1992 MTV Video Music Awards.

When a song becomes significant in the pop cultural zeitgeist, there is a very real danger that the song can supersede the songwriter or artist in the mind of the public, forever tying the artist's very identity to that one song or album. And then there are the expectations that naturally follow a hit. Once an artist hits on a winning formula, it's not long before fans, record labels, managers, agents, and critics alike begin to ask, "What's next?" This puts the artist in the unenviable position of chasing that next hit. Even a once-promising, innovative artist can fall into the cycle of trying to replicate and recapture the old magic.

When Boyz II Men released "End Of The Road" in the summer of 1992, they were in the midst of the last great era for R&B vocal groups. Alongside Boyz II Men, the early 1990s saw an influx of male and female vocal groups like En Vogue, Jodeci, TLC, Shai, Jade, Silk, SWV, Joe Public, and Mint Condition, who fused hip-hop with R&B while trying to carve out a space for themselves in the Black music market. This wealth of gifted young Black artists is now seen as a renaissance of sorts and really the last era in which vocal groups held any significant sway over the sound of contemporary R&B. Today, vocal groups have essentially disappeared, with solo artists dominating the R&B landscape. Historically and culturally, the R&B groups of the 1990s were perfectly situated to absorb and utilize

a number of key influences. Much like Boyz II Men, the members of these groups were Gen Xers who saw the rise of hip-hop culture firsthand, and by the time they were making music of their own, hip-hop had taken over as the predominant cultural movement among young Black Americans. Many of these groups were also likely influenced by the music of their youth and their parents' generation, the vocal groups of Motown, Stax, Philadelphia International, and the like.

With so many groups capturing the imagination of the masses and producing significant hits, R&B was a fiercely competitive field in the early 1990s. Boyz II Men's *Cooleyhighharmony* was already a hit, the album selling well initially and producing "Motownphilly" and "It's So Hard To Say Goodbye To Yesterday," singles that made it into the Top 5 of the *Billboard* Hot 100 in the United States. Then, in the summer of 1992, "End Of The Road" catapulted the band into a different stratum. So how does a group follow up the biggest song of the year?

As the previous chapter discusses, Boyz II Men were lucky to enter into a partnership with veteran hitmakers Jimmy Jam & Terry Lewis and one of the men who wrote "End Of The Road," Kenneth "Babyface" Edmonds, for their sophomore album, *II*. "End Of The Road" had proven that the group had profound chemistry with Babyface, and reuniting with the famed songwriter-producer for another big ballad seemed like a no-brainer. However, when Babyface pitched a song called "I'll Make Love To You" to the group, they were initially hesitant.

"After we did 'End Of The Road,' it certainly made sense that we got back together with them and did something else," Babyface said in a 2017 interview with *Songwriter Universe*. "I can remember what Jheryl Busby told me at the time. Initially, 'I'll Make Love To You' was voted off the album. I think it was, they thought it was too similar to the road they had already been down. But then Jheryl Busby made an executive call and [released it] anyway."

> *"We didn't understand how much of an impact the song was going to have. That's youth."*

In a 2017 interview with *Entertainment Weekly*, Shawn explained the group's position on the song. "The funny part is that we felt like it sounded too much like 'End Of The Road,'" he said. "We didn't want to do it." Shawn recalled in that interview that the group was "somewhat forced" to record the song, adding, "We didn't understand how much of an impact the song was going to have. That's youth."

Concerns about its similarities with "End Of The Road" aside, "I'll Make Love To You"

would prove to be the perfect follow-up single for the band. While tastes are ever-changing in the music scene, in 1994, there was still a demand for the kind of sweeping, heartfelt ballads that Boyz II Men had become known for. The charts were filled with songs like All-4-One's "I Swear" and Mariah Carey and Luther Vandross' cover of Diana Ross and Lionel Richie's "Endless Love." When "I'll Make Love To You" arrived in July 1994, the world was ready for the next "End Of The Road." What they got surpassed it.

The song opens at a slow, almost patient tempo. The song's kick, hi-hat, and rimshot pattern are reminiscent of the classic doo-wop ballads of the 1950s and the late-night slow jams of the 1970s. Like most Boyz II Men ballads, the bones of "I'll Make Love To You" share common DNA with the great R&B classics of the past. The rhythm section is rounded out by renowned session player Reggie Hamilton's melodic bassline. The synth brass and piano give the intro a regal, yet anticipatory, air. The references throughout Nate and Shawn's verses to candles, wine, and a warm fire make the song's intentions clear (if the title hadn't already): "I'll Make Love To You" is a song dedicated to the art of seduction.

Like any great pop song, "I'll Make Love To You" is lifted to another level when the chorus kicks in. Sung by the group in unison, the chorus harmonies are not as complex as

◄ Another candid shot from when the band was in Germany in 1992.

◄ Boyz II Men in the Netherlands in 1994.

we hear in some of the group's prior work, but the chorus has a distinct sing-along feel that makes it impossible to forget. Wanyá's voice soars through the bridge, jacking up the energy to unimaginable heights.

At first glance, it's easy to understand the band's original concerns about following up "End Of The Road" with another big ballad that treads similar musical territory. But "I'll Make Love To You" is subtly different than anything the group had done up to that point. *Cooleyhighharmony* had songs that occupied opposite ends of the spectrum in their approach to sex. Songs like "This Is My Heart" had a youthful, sentimental sense of romanticism, while "Uhh Ahh" was downright carnal. "I'll Make Love To You" occupies a space between the two and represents an evolution in the group's material. Specifically, the song's focus on the nonphysical aspects of seduction—setting the mood, making your partner feel desired, and making an effort to plan things out—is a mark of maturity. Babyface was in his mid-thirties when he wrote the song's lyrics, but it required nuance and power for the group of twentysomethings to deliver convincingly, and they pulled it off.

In an interview posted to the BoyzIIMenTV YouTube channel in 2011, Babyface recalled the first time he played "I'll Make Love To You" for the group. "It requires a certain kind of emotion that I feel like they're the only ones that can deliver it. Anyone else that does it, it just doesn't feel the same. The combination of their voices is what makes a difference. They

all need each other. It makes the gumbo perfect. I remember they came over to my house at the time and I played 'Water Runs Dry' for them because I wanted to do something kind of acoustic and they loved that one. That was immediate. 'I'll Make Love To You' was like my answer to 'End Of The Road' and I played it for them and they loved it but they felt like there was some hesitation about it."

> "['I'll Make Love To You'] requires a certain kind of emotion that I feel like they're the only ones that can deliver it. Anyone else that does it, it just doesn't feel the same. The combination of their voices is what makes a difference.

When "End Of The Road" broke Elvis' record for most consecutive weeks at No. 1 on the *Billboard* charts, it was an accomplishment that seemed unbeatable. Boyz II Men had pulled off a feat that seemed impossible to replicate, but "I'll Make Love To You" did just that. On August 13, 1994, "I'll Make Love To You" debuted at No. 5 on the *Billboard* Hot 100. That week, alt-rock singer-songwriter Lisa Loeb's lilting breakup song "Stay" held the No. 1 spot, but the momentum behind "I'll Make Love To You" sent it to No. 1 within three weeks. It held that position for a record-tying fourteen consecutive weeks. Much like "End Of The Road," the success of "I'll Make Love To You" inspired a campaign of live television appearances, award shows, talk shows, and the like. The group even made it back to *Top of the Pops*, performing the song via satellite from their hometown with a full band on the parkway by the Philadelphia Museum of Art.

With "I'll Make Love To You" still sitting atop the *Billboard* chart, Boyz II Men released another single in November 1994 that reinforced the group's dominance. "On Bended Knee" directly followed "I'll Make Love To You" up the charts upon its release on November 11, just like it did on the album's track list. "On Bended Knee" was the second single from *II* and one of the album's finest moments. While the production duos of Tim Kelley and Bob Robinson and the Characters (Troy Taylor and Charles Farrar) were gifted musicians and essential contributors to the album, the most experienced hitmakers to work on the *II* sessions were Jimmy Jam and Terry Lewis. In addition to working on "All Around The World," the pair wrote and produced "On Bended Knee." Working with them was also a full-circle moment for the group. Jam and Lewis had written and produced the New Edition song "Boys To Men" which inspired the group's name.

Opening with a wistful piano motif, "On Bended Knee" has a different feel than the Boyz II Men/Babyface ballads. The chords and overall atmosphere of the intro to "On Bended Knee" are similar to Force MDs 1985 ballad "Tender Love," another Jam and Lewis-written classic. Before the start of the first verse, it's clear that "On Bended Knee" represented a slightly different sound and

► Kim Fields in 1994, actress featured in the music video for "On Bended Knee" (1994).

feel than "End Of The Road" and "I'll Make Love To You." A dramatic piano turnaround plays before Shawn enters with the first verse, bringing the desperation of the lyrics to life with a tender and melancholic performance. Instead of complex runs and power, he opts for a kind of wounded delicacy in his vocal tone. This is the sound of a man who has been kicked around by love and taken to his breaking point. "On Bended Knee" wastes no time getting us to the song's indelible chorus.

> *Historically R&B has been a space where Black men could express a wider range of emotions, even those that fall outside the rigid confines of masculinity.*

It is this kind of lovelorn anguish that Boyz II Men have mastered throughout the years. It may seem over the top, but historically R&B has been a space where Black men could express a wider range of emotions, even those that fall outside the rigid confines of masculinity. The comedic trope of the "begging" male R&B singer wearing his heart and hurt on his sleeve is well known and the art of a man pouring his pain and desperation into the microphone is a cornerstone of the genre. The sensitivity and vulnerability required to write and perform a song like "On Bended

Knee" are luxuries not afforded to most Black men. Within these lyrics and voices lay emotional timbres that the twin prisons of race and gender have forbidden us to express.

Just past the song's midway point, Michael delivers a now-signature monologue. He is apologetic, regretful, and seeking forgiveness. Before the song ends, more promises are made, and we never get a resolution or a clear answer as to whether or not these men have been forgiven for their sins. The video for "On Bended Knee" hints at happier ends. Shot in New Orleans, the video finds each singer paired with a notable actress: Lark Voorhies, Renée Jones, Victoria Rowell, and Kim Fields. Mirroring the drama of the song, each couple struggles with assorted relationship strife, but they do ultimately reconcile.

Much like Boyz II Men's previous big ballads, "On Bended Knee" performed brilliantly on the charts. The song would eventually supplant "I'll Make Love To You" at the No. 1 spot on the *Billboard* Hot 100. With the potent combo of "I'll Make Love To You" with "On Bended Knee," as well as the previous success of "End Of The Road," the group was on a hot streak and it seemed like they could do no wrong. Boyz II Men would spend the rest of the 1990s navigating an increasingly volatile musical landscape. As popular trends fell out of favor and new trends emerged, the group would inevitably be set down the path of reinvention. But first, they had to pack up and hit the road.

BABYFACE AND THE
ART OF THE SONG

KENNETH "BABYFACE" EDMONDS IS A SONGWRITER'S SONG-
WRITER. THE SINGER/GUITARIST/PRODUCER IS ONE OF THE
MOST PROLIFIC AND SUCCESSFUL COMPOSERS OF HIS ERA. A
MULTIPLE GRAMMY AND AMERICAN MUSIC AWARD WINNER,
EDMONDS HAS PENNED COUNTLESS HITS FOR GENERATIONS OF
ARTISTS—AND FOR HIMSELF, AS A SOLO ARTIST.

Born in Indianapolis, Indiana, Edmonds grew up deeply embedded in the city's music scene. By the time he was a teenager, Edmonds was playing R&B in clubs around town.

In 2024, Babyface paid a visit to IPS Carl Wilde School 79 in Indianapolis to donate musical instruments to students as part of a partnership with the Music Will, a nonprofit that encourages young people to learn and pursue music. During the visit, Babyface spoke about the opportunities that Indianapolis' music scene afforded him as a kid and lamented the lack of venues for today's youth: "Those opportunities don't exist the same, as a matter of fact. There used to be clubs around for everybody to play, especially R&B. And I don't even know if that's true for even rock at this particular point."

Edmonds made his first serious splash in the Indianapolis music scene by singing and playing guitar in a local funk/soul band, Manchild. Following Manchild's breakup in 1979, Babyface had a short stint in a band called Crowd Pleasers, before joining Los Angeles-based R&B band the Deele. It was during this time that Edmonds met songwriter/producer L.A. Reid. The Deele had a few charting hits with songs like "Two Occasions," "Shoot 'em' Up Movies," and "Body Talk," but it was the partnership with Reid that made way for Edmonds' greatest successes.

By the late 1980s, L.A. Reid, Babyface, and Deele guitarist Daryl Simmons were turning out hit songs at an impressive rate, including the Whispers' "Rock Steady"; Bobby Brown's "Roni," "Every Little Step," and "Don't Be Cruel"; Karyn White's "Super Woman"; the Boys' "Dial My Heart"; and Babyface's own solo hits, "Tender Lover" and "Whip Appeal." The list of hit songs that the trio created at the time would make an unbeatable mixtape.

The 1990s brought more hits for Edmonds as he went on one of the greatest songwriting runs in the history of popular music. Babyface's songs—including Whitney Houston's "I'm Your Baby Tonight," Bobby Brown's "Humpin' Around,"

▼ Babyface at a Save the Music event in Washington, DC, in 1998.

TLC's "Baby, Baby, Baby," and Johnny Gill's "My, My, My"—dominated Black radio between 1990 and 1991. In the summer of 1992, Edmonds scored the biggest hit to date with Boyz II Men's smash ballad "End Of The Road."

"The first song I did with Boyz II Men was 'End Of The Road,' and that came from doing the Boomerang soundtrack," Babyface explained in a 2017 interview with Songwriter Universe. "It was our first major soundtrack that we did with our label [LaFace Records]. After watching the film, 'End Of The Road' was one of the songs that I had started to write. Then we did a demo of it, and we thought it would be a great idea to get Boyz II Men on it. So we sent the song to them, and they said, yes. So we ultimately went to Philadelphia, and we probably cut the song with them in three or four hours, because they were on the road and it was kind of in and out. At the time we did the song, it felt really great, but we had no idea that it was gonna do what it did."

In the summer of 1994, Boyz II Men released "I'll Make Love to You," another powerhouse, Babyface-penned ballad that spent fourteen weeks at No. 1 on *Billboard*'s Hot 100. In 1997, Boyz II Men followed up "End Of The Road" and "I'll Make Love to You" with "A Song For Mama," completing a trilogy of Boyz II Men/Babyface hits that set a standard for R&B balladry and rewrote the pop music record books.

In the 2000s, Babyface entered his fourth decade as a hitmaking songwriter/producer, racking up credits for Beyoncé, Mariah Carey, P!nk, Ariana Grande, Usher, Jay Z, TLC, and more. Edmonds' skill for crafting hits continued in recent years, when he cowrote SZA's 2023 No. 1 hit "Snooze" and appeared in NPR's popular Tiny Desk series, proving that his work still deeply resonated with contemporary audiences.

In a 2022 interview with DJ Booth, Babyface said, "I love working with artists and collaborating. Life, whether it's good or not, music is one thing you can always go to. It's healing. For me, the art of being able to still do music today and not be put in a bubble where I can't work on certain things because of how long I've been here . . . Doors have been opened for me to work with younger artists who still wanna work with me, that's my blessing."

CHAPTER 9

WE'RE JUST VIBIN'

THE SHIFTING SONIC LANDSCAPE

INETEEN-NINETY-FIVE IS RIGHT-fully viewed as a landmark year in hip-hop history. Even an incomplete list of classic albums released that year gives us some idea of how stacked the year was in terms of quality hip-hop music. Tupac Shakur's *Me Against The World*, Raekwon's *Only Built 4 Cuban Linx*, Mobb Deep's *The Infamous*, and Coolio's *Gangsta's Paradise* are just some of the impactful albums released that year that have gone on to become beloved classics.

◄ Boyz II Men in 1995.

The biggest rap albums of 1995 were high artistic achievements, and they all also sold well. Riding on the success of its multi-Platinum-selling title track, Coolio's *Gangsta's Paradise* went double platinum, and *Me Against The World* achieved that feat by the end of the year.

In just a few short years, the pop-rap stylings of MC Hammer, Vanilla Ice, and MC Brains had largely fallen out of favor. By 1995, the charts were filled with rappers that were far edgier than the decade's earlier pop-rappers, and it was clear that the genre had entered a new epoch. Rough, complex, and uncompromising rap records appealed to the masses and would go on to achieve status as commercial and critical darlings.

As the two reigning genres of Black popular music at the time, hip-hop and R&B's fates and many stylistic shifts had become interconnected. R&B acts had been inviting rappers to provide guest verses on songs since Chaka Khan and Melle Mel's 1985 collaboration on "I Feel For You." By the mid-1990s, the rap-meets-R&B collaboration was a common phenomenon, with Method Man and Mary J. Blige's "All I Need," Total and Notorious

B.I.G.'s "Can't You See," and Monica and Mr. Malik's "Like This And Like That" all charting in '95. Despite the growing popularity of hardcore hip-hop, rappers were still encouraged to collaborate with R&B singers to add a little "sweetness" to their tracks. The logic behind this practice was that R&B artists could smooth out a rap act's sound to court an even larger audience.

In 1995, Boyz II Men were without question one of the biggest acts in music, but they were not immune to the shifting sonic landscape around them. Hip-hop's slower, sample-based production had replaced the up-tempo, New Jack Swing-inspired jams that had ruled the late 1980s and early 1990s. As products of the hip-hop generation, fans and the industry likely expected that Boyz II Men would adjust to these changes. Exactly how they'd do it remained to be seen. But what better place to plot their future than a brand-new home base?

In March 1995, Boyz II Men finalized a lease agreement with Kajem, a recording studio in Gladwyne, Pennsylvania, a quaint suburban township about twelve miles outside Philadelphia. Established in 1977 by a group

◄ Boyz II Men with Mariah Carey, backstage at the 2001 Radio Music Awards.

147

► LL Cool J in 1995, who collaborated with Boyz II Men on the 1995 single "Hey Lover."

of producer/engineers—Mitch Goldfarb, Sam Moses, Kurt Shore, and Joe Alexander— Kajem had once hosted recording sessions for artists across the musical spectrum. Philly soul legend Patti LaBelle, heavy metal rockers Dream Theater, and Philly rap royalty like Tuff Crew and DJ Jazzy Jeff and the Fresh Prince all laid down tracks at the state-of-the-art space during its eighteen years in business. Before the building was converted into a recording studio, it had been a Civil War gun factory for local arms manufacturer Nippes and Company.

When Boyz II Men acquired the space from Goldfarb and Alexander, they rechristened it Stonecreek Recording Studios. Speaking to the *Philadelphia Inquirer* in the spring of 1995 about the new studio, Nathan explained, "We've always been on the lookout for a place outside of Philly where we can work without having to travel. This gives us a base for our creative projects."

"We've always been on the lookout for a place outside of Philly where we can work without having to travel. This gives us a base for our creative projects."

Although the group spent much of the year on tour, they still found time for those creative projects and new collaborations. In 1995, they released two singles that proved that the group were capable hitmakers both by themselves and with others: LL Cool J's "Hey Lover" and Mariah Carey's "One Sweet Day." If Boyz II Men represented one side of the 1990s pop-R&B spectrum occupied by groups that placed priority on intricate vocal harmony, Mariah Carey was the opposite side. A powerhouse soloist with an impressive five-octave vocal range, Carey spent the 1990s and 2000s burning up the charts alongside Boyz II Men. As the two most dominant acts in R&B and competitors on the charts, a collaboration may not have seemed inevitable, but musically, Mariah Carey and Boyz II Men were a match made in heaven.

"One Sweet Day" was created when Mariah Carey and producer/songwriter Walter Afanasieff began work on a song in tribute to her friend, music producer and C+C Music Factory founder David Cole, who passed away in February 1995. While working on the song, Carey felt that Boyz II Men's voices were the perfect ingredient to add to her heartfelt tribute.

"It was really the ultimate for me, to be able to get them to come and sing with me on that song," Carey said in an interview with VH1 shortly after the song was released, "because it just seemed like the chorus was crying out for their vocals."

At the time, Nate was also working on a song designed to pay homage to Khalil Rountree, their fallen mentor, following the group's memorial "Khalil (Interlude)" on *II*. In Jack Canfield, Mark Victor Hansen, and Jo-Ann Geffen's book *Chicken Soup for the Soul: The Story Behind the Song*, songwriters discuss the origins and meaning behind some of their most beloved compositions. In the book, Nate talked about how the song that would eventually become "One Sweet Day" came together.

"After [Rountree] died, I began working on a song for him while we were on the road," he explained. "Not too long after, we got a call from Tommy Mottola asking if we'd be interested in doing a duet with Mariah Carey. We went to the studio she was recording in at the Hit Factory in New York to hear the song they had in mind. She played us the melody and the hook, and it was amazing. It was almost the same song I was writing. I told her that I was working on a song with a similar melody and, while the lyrics were, of course, different, the premise was the same. They complemented each other. I sang to her the melody and lyrics of what I had written, and we merged the two. We switched things around to make them

work and wrote it that day. The other guys in the group filled in the holes to complete it."

By combining these two separate songs about friendship and loss, Carey and Boyz II Men produced a song that was more powerful than the sum of its parts. They recorded the song in just a few hours in between tour stops, and Boyz II Men and Mariah Carey had their next big hit on their hands. "One Sweet Day" was released in October 1995 and raced up the charts, securing multiple No. 1 positions in the US, including Pop Airplay, *Billboard* Hot 100, and Adult Pop Airplay. Certified 4x platinum to date, "One Sweet Day" was also No. 1 for sixteen consecutive weeks on the *Billboard* Hot 100.

In October of 1995, with yet another ballad ruling the charts, Boyz II Men released another collaboration that proved that the band could adapt to the ever-changing sound of hip-hop. "Hey Lover" was the first single released from LL Cool J's 1995 album, *Mr. Smith*. By 1995, LL was a certified veteran in the rap game and had already undergone several evolutions since his debut in 1984 at the age of sixteen. Following the lukewarm critical response to his 1993 album *14 Shots To The Dome*, *Mr. Smith* was set to be a return to form. An early pioneer of the hip-hop love ballad with songs like 1987's "I Need Love," LL Cool J had long tapped into the softer, romantic potential of rap music. By crafting songs that played up both his sensitivity and sex appeal, LL had struck upon a formula that especially appealed to young female rap fans. With love, romance, and sex as key aspects of his persona, it made perfect sense for the king of the rap love ballad to reach out to the reigning kings of the R&B ballad for his new album.

In 2012, LL Cool J told *Entertainment Weekly*, "I wrote this hook and I just thought it felt like Boyz II Men. They were on fire at the time, but more importantly, it just felt like they were made to do it. We drove out to Philly and I played the record for the guys. They got in the truck with me and some friends, and they loved it. We went right to the studio that night and I did the entire song in one take. Everything, it was just magical."

> *"I wrote this hook and I just thought it felt like Boyz II Men."*

Produced by the Trackmasters (hip-hop production duo Tone and Poke, aka Samuel Barnes and Jean-Claude Olivier), the song opens with a sped-up sample of the intro from Michael Jackson's "Lady In My Life," a two-bar loop of a synth and guitar lick that provided the song with an ethereal, dream-like foundation. Michael sets it off with a brief

monologue, informing a woman that he's had his eye on her, as the band backs him up with gorgeous harmonies while Shawn riffs and hits vocal runs. When the drums—sampled from Mary Jane Girl's "All Night Long"—kick in, LL starts his story of meeting and fantasizing about seducing a woman who is in a relationship with another man. The group rejoins on the chorus with a harmony part that blends perfectly. The chemistry between LL and Boyz II Men is seamless and the collaboration was both artistically and commercially successful. Upon release, "Hey Lover" peaked at No. 1 on the *Billboard* Hot Rap Songs chart in the US on its way to earning platinum certification.

The success of "Hey Lover" would be followed up by a Motown-produced project that label execs hoped would capitalize on the group's success and the changing sound of Black radio. About a month after "Hey Lover" debuted, Andre Harrell and Motown decided to release *The Remix Collection*—against the group's wishes. This act created a fissure that would ultimately grow into an irreparable rift between Boyz II Men and Motown.

At its core, the music industry revolves around the delicate dance between commerce and art. In the industry's best-case scenarios, artists are supported by the record companies that sign them, and that support allows them to create music that is both creatively fulfilling and commercially viable. At worst, the record

label acts as a loan shark, leveraging its power and influence to pervert the artist's vision in the interest of commerce. By all accounts, the relationship between Motown and Boyz II Men was not particularly problematic or adversarial. As a respected label with great significance to Black culture, Motown seemed like the perfect fit for Boyz II Men and for a while they were. An association with Motown lent status to the young group. While Boyz II Men were on their record-breaking run, both parties benefited greatly—and sold millions of records in the process.

Despite this fruitful partnership, there were signs that Motown was willing to contract the band's artistic vision and overrule them in key decisions about the music. One such incident came in 1994, when the band was working on *II*. Following the success of "End Of The Road," Motown was naturally on the hunt for a song from the group to repeat that success. Babyface was recruited to write and produce the new song, but after recording, the band felt it was too similar to "End Of The Road" and voted to leave it off the new album. Reportedly, Motown president Jheryl Busby made an executive power play and released the song against the band's wishes.

"I'll Make Love To You" went on to become a massive success, selling over one million copies in the US and putting radio in a chokehold for months. In this case, the record label's interference proved to be the right call from a commercial standpoint, and "I'll Make Love To You" still enjoys status as one of Boyz II Men's most beloved releases despite the group's initial hesitance.

It's easy to see what Motown was trying with their next decision, when they released *The Remix Collection* in the fall of 1995. Hip-hop was king and the band was on a red-hot streak of popular releases. It stood to reason that a fresh new collection of remixes by the biggest act in music would sell like hot cakes.

The Remix Collection is a compilation of songs from *Cooleyhighharmony* and *II*. With production primarily handled by Dallas Austin and Tim and Bob, the album occupies a curious sonic space between the New Jack Swing-inspired sound of the first album and a more contemporary hip-hop sound of 1994 and 1995. The album opens with "Countdown Interlude"/"Under Pressure (Dallas Austin Mix)"/"Sympin' Interlude," essentially a remixed medley of the up-tempo songs from *Cooleyhighharmony*. "Under Pressure" is beefed up with some nice Teddy Riley-style jazz piano comping, but Austin's remix doesn't really improve upon the original.

The group shot a video for Tim and Bob's breezy remix of "Vibin'" and recruited a handful of the top rappers in the game to drop guest verses. Method Man, Crack Mack, Treach from Naughty By Nature, and

Busta Rhymes, fresh from his show-stealing appearance on Mack's "Flava In Ya Ear" remix, all make appearances. The 12" single also featured another hip-hop-inspired remix of the song, the buttery Kenny "Smoove" Kornegay mix that featured Def Squad chief and former EPMD member, Erick Sermon, as well as Keith Murray, Redman, and 2 Ta Da Head. "I Remember" is another Tim and Bob-produced tune that taps into the chilled-out, mid-1990s hip-hop sound. Based around head-nodding drums, pitched-down electric piano, and a horn sample, the beat wouldn't have felt out of place on any number of underground rap records from 1995. Lyrically, Boyz II Men add a bit of venom to Tim and Bob's dark beat with lines admonishing an unnamed person trying to cozy up to the group and leech off their success. It's a decidedly mean-spirited and fussy angle for the group to explore, but not surprising that four young men who'd recently become

superstars had such concerns.

Babyface's "Strat Mix" of "Water Runs Dry" adds thicker drums, a g-funk-style synth line, and some Curtis Mayfieldesque guitar trills. The added production and instrumentation raises the track's energy, but it's not necessarily an improvement on the beloved ballad. "I'll Make Love To You (Make Love To You Version)" is a slick and novel take on the well-known hit. Unlike some of the other remixes on the album, every element of "I'll Make Love To You" is altered for this track. The lyrics are playfully changed, the rhythm section is bouncier, some trippy backward synths are added along with new keyboard line, and the vocal harmonies are reworked. The result is a daring and creative flip that solidifies Tim and Bob as the MVPs of this collection.

Curiously, Austin's next two tracks—"Uhh Ahh (Dedication Mix)" and "Motownphilly (Quiet Storm Version)"—add some cheesy synths that feel like they'd find use in a love

U KNOW

"I got it all together and coordinated everything. At the end of that thirty days, Boyz II Men had an open house and a who's who of everybody was there. Gamble and Huff and every huge celebrity was in the place." —George Hajioannou, audio engineer, on building and opening Stonecreek Studio

scene from a late 1980s action film. The contrast of quality and freshness between the Austin tracks and the Tim and Bob remixes is dramatic. One can't help but wonder how *The Remix Collection* would've turned out if the duo had been allowed to take the lead for the entire project. Despite having some great material to work with, the remixes of the *Cooleyhighharmony* tunes mostly fell flat. *Cooleyhighharmony* and *The Remix Collection* may have only been separated by four years, but at the rate that Black popular music was evolving at the time, the stylistic gulf between Boyz II Men's debut album and most recent work is more than noticeable.

It's unclear if Motown was aiming for any degree of sonic or stylistic cohesion when they compiled *The Remix Collection*. Perhaps the intended purpose of the project was to put a fresh spin in the band's catalog without concern for any overarching narrative or unified sound. Regardless, it is known that Boyz II Men did not approve of *The Remix Collection*.

In an interview with Record.net in the fall of 2004, Nate spoke candidly about the album. "I don't think it was creative," he told the outlet. "Our fans are our extended family, and I felt like the label was taking advantage of them to a degree to get as much money as they could while we were still popular. It wasn't a loyal thing to do."

Although *The Remix Collection* would eventually be certified platinum in 2012, the general consensus from fans and critics alike is perhaps best summed up by music journalist Patrick Rapa in his fantastic 2021 *Philadelphia Magazine* piece "Why, 30 Years Later, the World Still Loves Boyz II Men": "Clearly a strike-while-the-iron's-hot cash grab, the record takes tracks from *Cooleyhighharmony* and *II* and refurbishes them with hip-hop and New Jack Swing razzle-dazzle like horns and record scratches. The label released it despite Boyz II Men's protests that it was, per Reuters, 'unauthorized and sub-standard.'" Reiterating the album's lukewarm reception, Rapa quotes music critic J.D. Considine's complaint from a 1995 *Baltimore Sun* review that "Boyz II Men almost seem like guests on their own song."

In the midst of one of the greatest runs in the history of popular music, Boyz II Men found themselves in an unenviable position. The group had built something truly special with Motown, but now the trust in their relationship had been broken. Navigating both this hardship with their label and the next phase of the group's career was crucial as the music industry was about to undergo radical changes over the next few years. Like all great pioneers, Boyz II Men had carved out a significant path and a new crop of groups were prepared to follow—perhaps even surpass them.

► Boyz II Men attend the 22nd Annual American Music Awards in 1995.

A BEHIND-THE-SCENES
INTERVIEW WITH . . .

GEORGE HAJIOANNOU IS AN ENGINEER AND AUDIO WIZARD. THE GO-TO GUY FOR MUSICIANS AND STUDIOS LOOKING TO PUT TOGETHER RECORDING SPACES, HAJIOANNOU OVERSAW THE CONSTRUCTION OF BOYZ II MEN'S STONECREEK STUDIO ALONGSIDE HIS WIFE, STONECREEK'S MANAGER, DARIA MARMALUK-HAJIOANNOU.

▶ **HOW DID YOU FIRST START WORKING WITH BOYZ II MEN?**

I met Nate at Jazzy Jeff's house. Jeff was having a party get-together thing and he asked me to come over because he's a client of mine. He introduced me to Nate, and we started talking, and then Nate said, "I want to show you some stuff that I'm considering." So we went to the parking lot and Nate opened up this trunk. He showed me some gear he had. He was asking me about making them all work together.

▶ **OKAY. I'M CURIOUS, WHAT GEAR DID HE HAVE?**

It was a small mixer; it wasn't anything big. And I think this was just when they were just starting to make money. They had to hit [sales] thresholds and the record company didn't think they would hit these thresholds. And not only did they hit them, they surpassed them.

▶ **YEAH, I COULDN'T EVEN IMAGINE BEING IN A BAND AND THEN RELEASING A RECORD LIKE THAT [*II*] WITH THOSE MONSTER HITS ON IT.**

It was one after another after another, and there was a time if you looked at the Top 10, either they were in it or they had something to do with what was on there.

▶ **WHAT WAS IT LIKE WORKING WITH THEM DURING THAT TIME?**

I put the whole thing [Stonecreek Studio] together. And my wife was the one who was the business end of the whole thing. She just gave birth to my daughter and they were like, "Please, please, please, we need somebody that we can trust."

▶ **DID YOU PRIMARILY WORK WITH THEM IN AN ENGINEERING CAPACITY AT THEIR STUDIO OR WERE YOU WORKING WITH THEM IN INTEGRATING THE GEAR AND COORDINATING THE DESIGN?**

I was kind of like the foreman for the whole thing. But I think I was above and beyond that because they heavily depended on me to make everything happen. I spent a lot of time with Nate, a lot of time with Wanyá, and a little bit of time with Shawn, when I went to his house and talked with his mom. I had to put all the rooms together because all their offices were separate production suites. I got all the gear in there and made everything work.

▲ Boyz II Men in 1996, around the time they opened Stonecreek.

CHAPTER 10

ALL AROUND THE WORLD

HEADLINERS IN THEIR OWN RIGHT

W ITH THEIR GREAT SUCCESSES AND popularity, Boyz II Men were still working night to night on the road. The All Around the World Tour of 1995 was the group's first major outing as headliners. Covering roughly 130 dates in cities throughout the US and Canada, the tour not only tested the band members' stamina, it proved to be a test of their reach to audiences. Dominating radio and prestige award shows is one thing, but packing out arenas is another.

◄ Boyz II Men performing live in 1995 on their All Around the World Tour.

On January 15, 1995, Boyz II Men made a stop in Philly for a triumphant homecoming. With Brandy and Babyface in tow, the Sunday night show took place at the legendary South Philly venue, the Spectrum. In a review published on January 17, *Philadelphia Inquirer* staff writer Dan DeLuca had especially high praise for Babyface, calling him a "master showman," and remarked on Boyz II Men's beautiful singing that night. Interestingly, DeLuca noted that the audience of the sold-out, nineteen-thousand-seat show was "largely white, largely teenage," and "largely female," clearly a mark of the group's crossover appeal. Nearly thirty years later, it's difficult to gauge an accurate account of the tour's demographic composition, but it's safe to say that the group's music had attracted a significant number of white fans, whether intentionally or not.

Following the Philly show, the tour made stops in Massachusetts before swinging through North Carolina and Virginia. Following dates in Cleveland, Ohio; Anaheim, California; and San Jose, California, it was time for Boyz II Men to return to Los Angeles for the year's first round of major award shows.

In the winter of 1995, Boyz II Men found themselves with multiple nominations for their work on *II*. On January 30, the 22nd Annual American Music Awards were hosted at the Shrine Auditorium in LA and the group entered with four nominations to their name. "I'll Make Love To You" faced off against Ace Of Base's "The Sign" and Celine Dion's "The Power Of Love" for Favorite Pop/Rock Song. The group also secured a nomination for "I'll Make Love To You" for Favorite Soul/R&B Song, while the group was nominated alongside Salt-N-Pepa and Jodeci for Favorite Soul/R&B Band/Duo/Group. In a clear nod to the group's crossover appeal, they also went up against Michael Bolton and Mariah Carey for Favorite Adult Contemporary Artist. The group also performed at the show, singing a rousing version of "On Bended Knee" to waves of screams from audience members. Of all the artists nominated for American Music Awards that year, only Mariah Carey matched Boyz II Men in number of nominations, and the group won three awards (Michael Bolton was named the Favorite Adult Contemporary Artist).

The group was nominated for three Grammys that year, too, for Best R&B Performance by a Duo or Group with Vocal for "I'll Make Love To You," Best R&B Album for *II*, and the much coveted Record Of The Year. On award show night, Boyz II Men won Best R&B Performance by a Duo or Group and Best R&B Album.

At the 1995 Soul Train Music Awards, "I'll Make Love To You" grabbed a pair of nominations, winning Best R&B/Soul Single — Group, Band or Duo, and losing R&B/Soul or

▼ Shawn during a Boyz II Men
stop at 103 Radio Station in Atlanta
promoting their upcoming tour, 1995.

Rap Song Of The Year to Barry White's comeback hit, "Practice What You Preach." The video for the Wanyá and Brian McKnight-penned holiday gem "Let It Snow" from *Christmas Interpretations* was nominated for Best R&B/Soul or Rap Music Video but lost to Aaron Hall's "I Miss You." *II* won R&B/Soul Album of the Year – Group, Band or Duo. With this strong showing at an award show focused on Black music specifically, it was clear that despite Boyz II Men's crossover success, the group was still respected by their core R&B fanbase and Black industry professionals.

Two days after their appearance at the Soul Train Music Awards, Boyz II Men were back on the road for the All Around the World Tour. The tour spent the next week making stops across California—in San Diego, Reno, Fresno—and in Tacoma, Washington. In his review of the Tacoma show—which was hosted at the twenty-one-thousand-seat Tacoma Dome—*Seattle Times* writer Tom Phalen praised Boyz II Men's performance, with one glaring issue.

"They had all the moves: the dancing moves, the smoke, fire and special effects moves, the costume moves and the singing moves," Phalen wrote. "What they didn't have, for the first fifteen minutes of their set, was the sound moves. Between the constant roar of the audience and the Tacoma Dome's less-than-pristine acoustics, the

Men's signature vocals, that deft interplay and four-part harmony, were lost in the muddle. You could feel it and you could see it, but at times it was hard to identify."

> *"They had all the moves: the dancing moves, the smoke, fire and special effects moves, the costume moves and the singing moves."*

Phelan singled out "Motownphilly" as the highlight of the night, pointing to the band's showmanship and blending of styles: "One of the band's best numbers, 'Motownphilly' has punch, drive, glib rap and deft juke/jazz scat done in pristine harmony. True to what the sounds of Motown and Philadelphia have always meant to music and show business, it was an exhilarating blend of style and substance, of soulful sounds all dressed up. Only here it was Boyz II Men, the next generation with a new bag of tricks."

Following a swing around the Gulf region, the South, the Midwest, and the Northeast, the band landed in Washington, DC. On April 22, Boyz II Men performed at the National Earth Day Rally as part of a weekend of events that included acts like alt-rockers Toad The Wet Sprocket, Darius Rucker of Hootie and the

Blowfish, Kenny Loggins, Shawn Colvin, and others. Boyz II Men performed "Thank You," "It's So Hard To Say Goodbye To Yesterday," and a cover of the Beatles' "Yesterday."

With the All Around the World Tour moving steadily and the band still making stops for TV appearances, their schedule throughout 1995 was particularly grueling. In an interview for *Us II You*, the group talked about life on the road and how they relieved the pressure. Nate explained, "We keep it sane and fun on the road as much as we can. Playing sports, video games, writing music, shopping. We try to get away from the work." Shawn added, "Sometimes it feels as if we live together on the bus, traveling from city to city, driving all night long. We could be arguing really deep about girls or whatever and we start to laugh like it's the most ridiculous thing. It's like in a family."

> *"Sometimes it feels as if we live together on the bus, traveling from city to city, driving all night long. We could be arguing really deep about girls or whatever and we start to laugh like it's the most ridiculous thing. It's like in a family."*

June brought another round of award show appearances. The Blockbuster Entertainment Awards, MTV Movie Awards, and VH1 Honors all taped within a three-week span, and each featured performances by the group. At the VH1 Honors, Morgan Freeman presented Michael Jackson with the Humanitarian Award for his achievements with the Heal The World Foundation, and Boyz II Men sang a cover of Jackson's song "Heal The World." Jackson then joined Boyz II Men on stage for a spirited version of "We Are The World."

This would not be the only meeting between Boyz II Men and Michael Jackson that year. The group contributed some background vocals to the title track "History" from Jackson's album *HIStory - Past, Present And Future - Book 1*. When asked about their relationship with Jackson during a 1995 segment for VH1, Shawn spoke of the group's shared admiration for the King of Pop: "This is the guy that we all looked up to. We couldn't help but look up to him. And still do in a lot of ways. We never imagined that we'd even meet him and to have him ask us to be on his album, it's a true honor."

On June 23—the day after the VH1 Honors—Boyz II Men landed in Miami to join the Budweiser Superfest, a popular national tour sponsored by the beer company. Boyz II Men headlined the twenty-three-date tour with acts like TLC, Montell Jordan, and Mary

▲ Boyz II Men posing with their Grammys for Best R&B Album and Best R&B Performance by a Group at the 37th Annual Grammy Awards in 1995.

▼　Boyz II Men at the Soul
Train Music Awards in 1995.

J. Blige. Blackstreet, as well as R&B veterans like Anita Baker, Frankie Beverly and Maze, and Gerald Levert also joined the tour for a handful of dates.

Going Home is a televised concert film, originally aired on the Disney Channel, that filmed the final date of the Budweiser Superfest. Shot on Sunday, August 27, 1995, at the world-famous Alamodome in San Antonio, Texas, the concert film opens with a shot of Boyz II Men backstage, dressed in all white and holding hands in a prayer circle. The shot of the prayer is overlaid with images and audio of fans screaming in anticipation. It's clear that the screams are meant to be energizing, getting us ready for the show, but they're also intrusive, threatening to drown out this private, quiet moment. Each member makes their way to the stage and stands completely still while the crowd goes wild. A wall of fiery pyrotechnics suddenly go off and the band then kicks into a flashy, high-energy intro, before quickly segueing into "U Know," followed by "Little Things." The strategy here is clear: The group is ambushing the audience with a barrage of up-tempo tunes before taking them into deep waters with their emotionally devastating ballads.

About ten minutes in, when the backing band launches into "Your Love," the quartet are already drenched in sweat. After the show's relentless pace for the opening, everything slows down for "Please Don't Go," with Shawn stepping to the front to sing lead while Michael, Wanyá, and Nate pull off some vintage Temptations/Spinners-style choreography. Reflecting some of the band's core influences, the choreography throughout *Going Home* sits somewhere between 1960s and 1970s soul-influenced synchronized steps and hip-hop, a young group at the height of their powers calling back to the great performers of the past. The steps, the vocals, and the overall presentation remind us that Boyz II Men are a part of a grand tradition that stretches back into the recesses of Black music history.

The ballad section of the concert is particularly strong, as the band runs through fiery versions of "On Bended Knee," "50 Candles," "I'll Make Love To You," and "Water Runs Dry." Following the suite of slow songs, the band changes tempo (and outfits) for performances of "Thank You" and "Motownphilly." The show climaxes with a rollicking take on the band's career-defining hit "End Of The Road." By picking up the song's tempo and adding a few instrumental flourishes, the backing band injects some muscle into the song. Atop a steady wall of screams from the fans, the group play with the song's melody, improvising runs and adding new melodic elements to the then-familiar hit. Clocking in at a little over an hour, *Going Home* is a revelation and an incredible record of the complex and physically and emotionally intense performance the group was putting on night after night.

Following the San Antonio show, Boyz II Men made their way back east. On August 30, the group returned to play the Great Allentown Fair, in the small city of Allentown, Pennsylvania, about an hour outside Philly. In a concert review published by *The Morning Call*, journalist Sophia Lezin noted, "How quickly things change. When Boyz II Men last performed at an Allentown Fair concert in 1992, they were supposed to be the act to prep the crowd for the headliner, MC Hammer. While Hammer's career plummeted seemingly overnight, and the mention of his name is now relegated to jokes, Boyz II Men's popularity has mushroomed, defying the naysayers who thought they couldn't possibly top the success of their debut album, *Cooleyhighharmony*."

The next stop on the tour was the Montage Mountain Performing Arts Center in Scranton, Pennsylvania. The band and their opener, Montell Jordan, weathered storms to perform in front of an estimated ten thousand fans. Through September, Boyz II Men boomeranged back across the country and then up to Vancouver, British Columbia; Edmonton, Alberta; Anchorage, Alaska; and the Pacific Northwest. The trail of reviews by local papers of these concerts all paint a similar picture: Boyz II Men played a litany of

hits while the arenas lit up with thunderous screams and applause.

These tour stages were not the only place where fans could hear the group. In the fall of 1995, Motown released a compilation album dedicated to the life and work of R&B legend and Motown scion, Marvin Gaye. The album, *Inner City Blues (The Music Of Marvin Gaye)*, featured contemporary acts reinterpreting some of Gaye's most famous songs. The album opens with his daughter, Nona Gaye, performing an ethereal version of the title track, "Inner City Blues (Make Me Wanna Holler)." On a track list that includes the likes of Madonna (paired with the band Massive Attack, no less), Stevie Wonder, Lisa Stansfield, Bono, and Digable Planets, Boyz II Men bring their affinity for vocal harmony to their funky cover of "Let's Get It On." Produced by Keith Crouch, the buttery smooth cover is based around a mid-tempo groove, electric piano, and guitar.

While the music and tours were firing on all cylinders, a shake-up at Motown's executive level would create serious friction between Boyz II Men and the label that helped make them stars. On October 2, 1995, Andre Harrell replaced Jheryl Busby as the CEO of Motown. Busby, who had taken over the label after Berry Gordy sold it in 1988, was an old-school record man, having cut his teeth working for labels like Casablanca, MCA, and legendary Memphis Soul imprint Stax Records. Harrell's

▼ Jheryl Busby (left)
with Diana Ross in 1993.

music-business journey was quite different. Born in the Bronx in the 1960s, Harrell was 11 years Busby's junior and had come up under the influence of a radically different cultural milieu. Harrell's first foray into the music business was not as an executive, but as an artist. In the early 1980s, he released several records under the name Dr. Jeckyll as part of the rap duo Dr. Jeckyll and Mr. Hyde. From there, Harrell formed his own label, Uptown Records, a wildly successful endeavor with a packed stable of talent including Mary J. Blige, Heavy D & the Boyz, Jodeci, and more. Notably, Sean Combs worked as an intern at Uptown before Harrell fired him in 1993, which forced Combs to start his own label, Bad Boy Records.

With Harrell's background as an artist and credibility in both hip-hop and contemporary R&B, one might assume he'd be the perfect candidate to guide the next chapter of Boyz II Men's career. By all accounts, this was not the case. As Harrell reflected later in an interview with writer Adam White, "If it was me and the team that had made me successful was no longer there, and a new team was coming in, I figure it would create a little uncertainty until the [new] team is complete and there's success."

If the band was truly upset with Harrell being hired, that displeasure was exacerbated with Harrell's decision to release *The Remix Collection*, the album of Boyz II Men remixes, against their will. While the Boyz II Men remixes had plenty of musical value and novel ideas, the project's release set in motion the slow dissolution of the group's relationship with Motown.

U KNOW

"I lived in Harlem at the time [of *Cooleyhighharmony*'s release] and you'd walk down the street and hear somebody blasting Boyz II Men. As much as I loved 'Motownphilly,' I think I loved 'It's So Hard To Say Goodbye To Yesterday' even more. I grew up in the '70s and saw *Cooley High* when it came out, so that song resonated with me." —*Michael Gonzales, music journalist*

BOYZ II MEN GOES HOLLYWOOD

AT THE HEIGHT OF THEIR FAME IN THE 1990S, BOYZ II MEN'S MUSIC REACHED A DEGREE OF UBIQUITY THAT FEW GROUPS HAVE RIVALED. SELLING MILLIONS OF RECORDS, BREAKING HISTORIC RECORDS ON THE BILLBOARD CHARTS, AND COLLECTING ARMFULS OF TROPHIES, BOYZ II MEN DOMINATED THE MUSIC WORLD AT THAT TIME.

As a result of their popularity, the group found themselves making headway in other areas of entertainment. While it was common for Nate, Shawn, Wanyá, and Michael to make appearances on late-night talk shows like *The Arsenio Hall Show*, *The Late Show with David Letterman*, and *The Tonight Show with Jay Leno* in the 1990s, the group also made some memorable appearances on television and in film soundtracks.

The group made its first major foray into show business in 1992 with "End Of The Road," a certified hit written for the *Boomerang* soundtrack. The song shot them into the stratosphere of fame and visibility, and the success of the song and the film made Boyz II Men a go-to choice for movie soundtracks of the day. Boyz II Men's next big soundtrack hit came in 1997, when "A Song For Mama," a loving ballad, appeared in the family drama *Soul Food*. In 1998, the group was included on the soundtrack for the Disney animated feature *Prince of Egypt* with "I Will Get There." Written by legendary songwriter Diane Warren, "I Will Get

There" is a soaring, triumphant ballad which the group recruited their old collaborators Jimmy Jam and Terry Lewis to produce.

In 1992, the same year as *Boomerang*'s release, the group appeared in the television series *The Jacksons: An American Dream*. A dramatic and harrowing series, the show detailed the Jackson family's struggles under their abusive father, Joe Jackson, and the Jackson 5's meteoric rise to fame. Boyz II Men made a brief appearance in the show, singing a beautiful a cappella version of the Five Satins' 1956 doo-wop classic, "In The Still of The Night." Boyz II Men also made a guest appearance on a 1993 Christmas episode of *The Fresh Prince of Bel Air*, showing off a comedic rapport with Will Smith and singing the holiday classic "Silent Night."

The group has also performed live on countless occasions, beyond their tour and concert performance. On March 28, 1999, Boyz II Men returned to Philly for WrestleMania XV at the First Union Center (now the Wells Fargo Center),

opening the annual professional wrestling extrav-
aganza with an understated, elegantly harmonized
version of "America the Beautiful."

Boyz II Men songs that were once fresh hits
have now matured and become accepted as
standards. This fact is evidenced by how many
younger performers employ them in popular tele-
vision singing competitions like *American Idol*,
X Factor, *The Voice*, and beyond. Whether it's
"Motownphilly" showing up on the popular *Grand
Theft Auto San Andreas* video game in the 2000s
or their hilarious 2023 appearance on *The Late
Show with Stephen Colbert* where they remixed "I'll
Make Love To You (But We Don't Have To)," Boyz
II Men's songs are still beloved and ever-present.

CHAPTER 11

FULL CIRCLE

THE NEXT *EVOLUTION* OF BOYZ II MEN

AFTER THE WHIRLWIND OF EXTENSIVE touring in 1995 that followed the success of *II*, Boyz II Men hunkered down at their recording studio, Stonecreek, and got to work on new music. In a 1996 interview with the *Philadelphia Daily News*, Wanyá said that the band initially had plans to take a break that year. "This was supposed to be our year off from touring and recording, but we've been pretty busy," he related. It'd be natural to assume that pressure from the powers at Motown is what brought the band back into the studio, but in the same *Daily News* piece, Shawn pushed back against this assumption, saying, "They want us to take our time and make sure it's up to par."

◀ Boyz II Men posing in 1996.

▼ Boyz II Men Boulevard Street
Renaming Ceremony in 2017.

In addition to the time spent recording *Evolution*, 1996 was an eventful year for Boyz II Men. In January, "One Sweet Day" was nominated for two Grammy awards, Record of the Year, and Best Pop Collaboration with Vocals. Later in the month, the band won Favorite Soul/R&B Band/Duo Group and Favorite Soul/R&B Album at the American Music Awards. In February, the Philadelphia Music Alliance announced that the band would be the youngest recipients of a star on Philadelphia's Music Walk of Fame, located along Broad Street. The band was honored in a class that included Joan Jett, the Intruders, legendary drummer Philly Joe Jones, guitarist Pat Martino, Philly Pops conductor Peter Nero, and Philadelphia Orchestra conductor William Smith. During this time, the band also briefly tried their hands as record executives. Following the success of "One Sweet Day," Mariah Carey's then-husband and Epic Records head honcho, Tommy Mottola, offered the band their own imprint label: Stonecreek Records. With all this activity surrounding the band during what was supposed to be their down-time, Boyz II Men got to work on the album that would become *Evolution*.

Mostly recorded at Stonecreek, *Evolution* doubles down on the soulful R&B sound that Boyz II Men were known for. Hip-hop, rock, and high-energy pop may have been ruling the charts, but the Boyz stayed true to the sound that brought them to the proverbial "dance" of fortune and fame. The production lineup on the album was stacked, with Sean "Puff Daddy" Combs' Hitmen stable credited alongside Babyface, Keith Crouch, Durrel L. Bottoms, Jimmy Jam and Terry Lewis, and Boyz II Men themselves. *Evolution* opens with "Doin' Just Fine," a lush and melancholy breakup song that reminds us that there is a way forward after a relationship has ended. In traditional Boyz II Men fashion, the song's simple chorus is augmented with a dense wall of vocal harmonies. While *Evolution* did feature a few up-tempo, hip-hop-influenced songs, opening with "Doin' Just Fine" sent a clear message: The world's greatest balladeers are still here and pushing what they do best to the forefront.

If audiences in 1997 thought that Boyz II Men had run out of ways to sing about the intricacies and challenges of love, they were in for a pleasant surprise. Babyface returned for the ballad "Never," a slow-tempo song with an uplifting chorus in line with other Babyface-penned ballads. A subtle touch was added to the song's arrangement with the inclusion of an electric sitar reminiscent of Bobby Eli's sound on "You Make Me Feel Brand New" and "You Are Everything" by Philly soul legends the Stylistics. With just its first two tracks, a theme begins emerging for *Evolution*. The band is wrestling with the implications of life after heartbreak and offering crucial insights on how to heal and move forward.

Fan favorite "4 Seasons Of Loneliness" is up third on the track list, written and produced by Jimmy Jam and Terry Lewis. The song opens with piano, organ, and a bouncy, electronic drumbeat played at half-time, taking us through the grief and time it takes to get over a lost love. Babyface returns for a pair of beautifully written songs, "Girl in the Life Magazine" and "A Song For Mama." The first song is a tale of love guided by fate and chance, while the latter is a beautiful, piano-backed ballad and a high point on *Evolution*. (It also made an appearance on the soundtrack of the 1997 film *Soul Food*.) "A Song For Mama" is a refreshing exploration of familial love, as the group's members were primarily raised by their mothers and maintained close relationships with them.

Notably, the group returns to their roots on *Evolution* with an a cappella cover of New Edition's "Can You Stand The Rain," performing a restrained and powerfully understated version of the song. The leads are dynamic and impassioned, and the backing harmonies amount to a full and dynamic musical arrangement without the aid of any instrumentation. The power and attention to detail the group bring is formidable, and the subtle changes to the arrangement and delivery reveal a true familiarity and command of the song. If the group brought even a portion of this kind of singing to that initial audition back in 1989, it's easy to see why Michael Bivins was so impressed with them.

Sean Combs and Ron "Amen-Ra" Lawrence of Bad Boy Records' Hitmen production team were recruited to produce the up-tempo R&B jam "Can't Let Her Go." With its danceable beat and funky guitars, the song is an anomaly in the group's catalog up to that point, a full-on swing for the attention of the era's DJs, and it works well. "Baby C'mon" is another standout, with Keith Crouch bringing a bouncy harpsichord and wah-wah-laced beat and the group's lyrics going into full-on seductive mode. The next track, "Come On," was coproduced by Combs and cowritten by rising star Missy Elliott. Both "Come On" and "Baby C'mon" sound fresh and more contemporary for 1997 than anything else on the album. "Come On," especially, bears Elliott's melodic style and the production has that kind of nimble, double-time beat that Elliott and her partner, Tim "Timbaland" Mosley, were using to reshape the sound of R&B that year.

Evolution closes with "Dear God," an ambitious meditation on life and faith. For each section of the song, each member address God directly, admitting their personal failings

▼ Boyz II Men on the red carpet of the 23rd Annual American Music Awards in 1996, having won Favorite Soul/R&B Band/Duo Group and Favorite Soul/R&B Album.

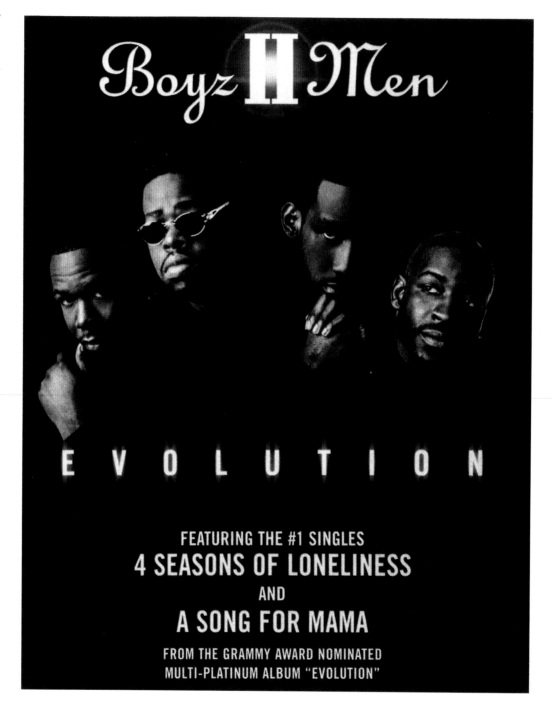

and expressing their gratitude with equal sincerity. As the group arrives at the chorus, the string section swells and the song blossoms, revealing itself as a pure expression of spiritual love between creator and creation. At its core, "Dear God" is a devotional hymn. The group's members had always discussed their faith in interviews, but the sentiment as it's expressed here further distinguished them from their peers.

The great takeaway from *Evolution* was that the four men that made up Boyz II Men were full, multidimensional human beings, with love, loss, sex, faith, and the fullness of the human experience displayed through the songs. Commercially, *Evolution* has been certified 2x platinum in the US, Japan, and Canada. The album may not have produced any record-shattering singles on par with "End Of The Road" or "I'll Make Love To You," but it still did well, especially considering how rapidly the music business was changing around the group. The next few years saw an explosion in pop music and a boom in the record industry. Bolstered by the sale of CDs in particular, the period from 1998 to 2000 marked the most profitable time on record for the music business. A new wave of Boyz II Men-inspired bands would prove to be both catalysts and beneficiaries of this coming boom period.

Before Chris Kirkpatrick founded the multi-Platinum, era-defining boy band, NSYNC, he worked as a singer in a doo-wop band called the Hollywood Hi-Tones. After graduating high school in 1990, Kirkpatrick moved from Dalton, Ohio, to Orlando, and made ends meet by bussing tables at Outback Steakhouse and singing with the Hi-Tones at Orlando's Universal Studios. A passionate singer and the son of a single mother who worked as a vocal coach, Chris was enamored with the harmonies of contemporary R&B groups of the day. By 1991, Boyz II Men made their debut with "Motownphilly." By combining R&B vocal harmonies with a hip-hop-influenced image and production, Boyz II Men changed the idea of what a contemporary male vocal group could be. The formula that the four guys from Philly carved out would have an immeasurable impact on Kirkpatrick, his future band, and the wave of boy bands that came along with them. In a 2024 interview with Fox17's Rock & Review show, Kirkpatrick said. "The doo-wop stuff . . . I fell into it because I loved it. It was all those harmonies and I was still doing a cappella groups on the side and that's what NSYNC kinda turned into. I was doing these a cappella groups and I'd arrange all these different pieces of music and I'd find everything from Az Yet, Boyz II Men, Take 6, all these bands that were doing these harmonies."

In 1995, Kirkpatrick met Lou Pearlman,

a music manager and record producer also living in Orlando at the time. Pearlman was the money and strategic mind behind the Backstreet Boys, a five-man vocal group who were gearing up to release their debut album on Jive Records. Pearlman had modeled the Backstreet Boys concept on New Kids On The Block, the Boston boy band put together in the early 1980s by former New Edition manager-producer, Maurice Starr. Having already secured a record deal for Backstreet Boys, Pearlman was confident that he could build another group using the now tried-and-true boy band formula. Kirkpatrick initially recruited JC Chasez and Justin Timberlake to join the group that he and Pearlman were putting together. Later, Joey Fatone and Lance Bass came into the fold, and NSYNC was born.

As Pearlman was putting together NSYNC and developing Backstreet Boys, Boyz II Men were inarguably the most popular vocal group on the planet. By selling millions of records and racking up industry accolades and awards off the strength of well-crafted songs sung by gifted vocalists, Boyz II Men carved a new lane that made it possible for R&B vocal groups to attain pop star status. Although Boyz II Men formed organically, with the four core members meeting and forming a deep musical connection at CAPA, they still helped show

ambitious men like Pearlman what was possible. NSYNC and the Backstreet Boys were the first experiments in the burgeoning Lou Pearlman boy band factory, but over the next decade, he would develop multiple groups including O-Town, LFO, Take 5, Natural, and many others, to varying degrees of success. By 1995, New Kids On The Block's time in the sun had come to an end, and Pearlman was developing Backstreet Boys to fill the void that NKOTB left.

With hardcore hip-hop and adult-themed alternative rock albums like Alanis Morissette's *Jagged Little Pill* and the Smashing Pumpkins' *Mellon Collie and the Infinite Sadness* ruling the charts, that void was evident. In both rock and hip-hop, decades of momentum eventually brought each respective genre's underground sound and aesthetic to the mainstream. In 1995, a band like Sonic Youth, who'd once toiled in New York's avant-garde art and punk scenes, was now being played daily on MTV, while a formerly underground rap act like Bone Thugs-n-Harmony made it to the Grammys stage. Popular music was growing up and there was a growing need for the kind of fun, teen, and pre-teen-focused pop that New Kids On The Block were known for and that the Pearlman bands perfected.

With Backstreet Boys and NSYNC emerging as the two new major players

▶ Backstreet Boys in 1996.

in pop music in the late 1990s, it became increasingly clear that the landscape was changing once again. On September 14, 1998, a little over a year after the release of *NSYNC* and *Backstreet's Back* (Backstreet's sophomore album), MTV's new video countdown show, *Total Request Live (TRL)* premiered. Fans would call into an MTV hotline or vote online for their favorite music video and the show would tally those votes and compile a countdown of the 10 most popular videos. Although the process's legitimacy would be called into question later, with accusations of record label's adding extra votes in favor of certain acts, the show was initially advertised as "democratic," and the purpose of *TRL* was to accurately reflect the tastes of young music fans. The show would also come to be synonymous with the rise of the boy band era in the late 1990s and early 2000s—perhaps because the top two videos on that first episode were NSYNC's "Tearin' Up My Heart" at No. 2 and Backstreet Boys' "I'll Never Break Your Heart" at No. 1. It was abundantly clear that as far as male vocal groups were concerned, the balance of power and popularity had shifted significantly, and Boyz II Men—the band that directly influenced these new acts—was left to figure out how to navigate this new landscape.

With the boy bands that they influenced asserting their dominance on the charts and selling a ton of records, it made sense that Boyz II Men would eventually be compared to their successors. In an ABC interview from September 2000, ahead of the release of *Evolution*'s follow-up, *Nathan Michael Shawn Wanya*, Shawn was asked about the boy band phenomenon and how Boyz II Men fit alongside those groups. "We've seen and heard a lot of interviews from a lot of the boy groups, and they [say] we inspired them to do what they do, and that's cool," he said. "But when we first came out that phrase 'boy band' was never used to describe us. A boy band has to fit in a certain category, and I don't think we fit in any of those categories."

> *"We've seen and heard a lot of interviews from a lot of the boy groups, and they [say] we inspired them to do what they do, and that's cool. But when we first came out that phrase 'boy band' was never used to describe us. A boy band has to fit in a certain category, and I don't think we fit in any of those categories."*

▼ Boyz II Men in
London, England for a
music video shoot in 1997.

Shawn was complimentary of boy bands like Backstreet Boys and NSYNC, assuring viewers that Boyz II Men didn't see them as competitors. "It's always nice to know that we've inspired some pretty famous folks right now. There's really no competition because, to be honest, they're very successful and they're selling a lot of records and selling a lot of tickets." Shawn closed out the interview with some more kind words and valuable advice for the up-and-coming groups: "We've met all of them, and everybody seems to be cool. They ask us a lot of questions, and the main thing I tell them is have fun, enjoy it, do all the things you guys want to do—go on tour, take pictures, all of that stuff. Remember it. Enjoy this moment."

In a cruel twist of irony, the same year that music revenue reached its peak, the peer-to-peer file trading program Napster went online. Napster's debut on June 1, 1999, dovetailed with the growing popularity of the MP3 and the spread of consumer internet accessibility. Though it would take a few years for these technological innovations to erode the profitability of music, it was evident that a storm was brewing. Throughout the 2000s, the record business' profitability steadily declined from the apex that it reached in 1999, and both new and veteran acts were left trying to figure out what to do next.

U KNOW

"Listening on repeat, I would sit and imagine the Girl in *Life Magazine* floating through the streets of Madrid. Black wavy hair, caramel skin, flowing red skirt, shopping for fruit at a street market before stepping back into her picture. Boyz II Men told the kinds of stories that allowed my brain to dream bigger than the places I had been, and now, I get to write songs that do the same." —*Loren Davis-Stroud, singer-songwriter*

RECORD YOUR SONG
AT STONECREEK

IN THE SUMMER OF 1995, AT THE HEIGHT OF THEIR FAME, BOYZ II MEN ANNOUNCED THE "RECORD YOUR SONG AT STONECREEK" TALENT SEARCH. THE GROUP PARTNERED WITH THE BIG BROTHERS/BIG SISTERS ORGANIZATION WITH THE HOPE OF IDENTIFYING AND HIGHLIGHTING TALENTED YOUNG PEOPLE WHO COULD USE A BIG BREAK.

The contest of course had some ground rules: Artists and all group members had to be under 25 years old and from the Philadelphia area, and the song submitted had to be an original work. The winner would have their original song professionally produced at Boyz II Men's Stonecreek Studio.

Contestants sent in demo tapes of their songs and Big Brothers/Big Sisters selected the ten best entries. Boyz II Men and their team then made their final selections from that top ten.

Stonecreek's studio manager, Daria Marmaluk-Hajioannou, remembers the contest fondly. The group members didn't just passively judge the quality of the tapes, they gave feedback and constructive criticism to contestants.

"The guys were so supportive, and people sent in their tapes and they were really encouraging," Marmaluk-Hajioannou says. "It was like 'You've got some great ideas, there's some great energy. Listen to the kind of music that's hitting, that you like, and try to see the difference between that and your demo and that's how you get to the next level.' They were always ready to give back. I'd worked with other celebrities who wouldn't give people the time of day. They were good souls."

▲ Boyz II Men photographed
in Los Angeles in 1997.

CHAPTER 12

NATHAN MICHAEL SHAWN WANYA

THE DAWN OF THE NEW MILLENNIUM

AS THE 1990S GAVE WAY TO THE 2000S, the R&B-influenced music of boy bands like NSYNC and the Backstreet Boys had fully asserted its command over the pop music landscape. In addition to these wildly successful boy bands, female pop artists like Britney Spears and Christina Aguilera shared custody of the top slots on the charts throughout the era.

◄ Boyz II Men at a Grammys pre-party in 2001.

▲ Jill Scott performs
in 2005.

Despite pop music's predominance, mainstream music in the early 2000s was still a wildly diverse affair. Hip-hop had fully completed its integration into the mainstream. The genre's increased visibility and the corporate investment not only raised the financial stakes for rap music but played a crucial role in shifting the actual sound of the music. Major mainstream rap artists like Nelly, Eminem, and Ja Rule were all gifted lyricists, but the climate of the day required that skill to be tempered with accessible songs and catchy, memorable hooks. Just as rap music had made a concerted effort to move closer to R&B in the early 1990s, by the early 2000s, it had chosen pop as its latest bedfellow. R&B experienced a creative renaissance on the periphery of the mainstream in that era, with the neo-soul movement. With their focus on rich 1970s funk, and soul-inspired live instrumentation, neo-soul artists like D'Angelo, Erykah Badu, Jill Scott, and Musiq Soulchild made records that were successes both creatively and commercially.

Despite the relative artistic health of the record business in the 2000s, the decade would be marked by an unprecedented downturn in music's profitability.

On October 2, 2000, hearings for the landmark case of *A&M Records v. Napster Inc.* began in the United States Court of Appeals for the Ninth Circuit. Napster was a peer-to-peer file trading site founded in 1999 by Shawn Fanning and Sean Parker. By allowing music fans to share and download small, compressed digital copies of their favorite songs, consumer acquisition of music was no longer reliant on the purchase of physical media—especially since Napster allowed users to illegally copy copyrighted musical works, which users then shared and downloaded widely for free. By 2001, Napster filed for bankruptcy and agreed to settle with copyright holders, but peer-to-peer file sharing was already radically altering the music business. Nearly one year after the *A&M Records v. Napster Inc.* hearings, Apple introduced the first iPod, ushering in the digital era of music.

When music industry profits soared in the late 1990s, the bulk of those profits came from the sale of CDs. CDs offered consumers superior audio quality than their predecessor, the cassette tape. The iPod was a hyper-portable device with relatively good sound (depending on the MP3 file) and could hold about one thousand songs in its 4"x2" frame. Between Napster, MP3s, and the iPod, a perfect storm of technological innovations had hit the music market, and record labels were not adequately prepared to face it. By 2003, profits were in a steady downward trend, with the total revenue for recorded music coming in just under $20 billion compared to its apex of $26.7 billion in 1999. Also in 2003, the Recording Industry Association of America—the trade organization that represents major American labels—filed 261 lawsuits against file-trading fans in federal courts across the nation.

This was a difficult period for artists as well. The musical and economic dynamics of the record business were fundamentally different than when Boyz II Men made their debut in the early 1990s. With their greatest commercial successes behind them, the group weathered label strife and a lineup change before charting a course for longevity in a fickle and ever-changing industry.

Following Universal Music Group's purchase of Motown's parent company, Polygram, Boyz II Men released their next album on Universal. That album, *Nathan Michael Shawn Wanya*, was released in the fall of 2000 and found the group adapting to the sound of the early millennium enthusiastically, but with varying degrees of success. Throughout the album, the group experiments with Latin-flavored arrangements and up-tempo electronic beats alongside the more traditional ballads that were the band's bread and butter. Songs like the groovy two-stepper, "Step On Up," "I Finally Know," and the album's closer, "Do You Remember," were clear standouts, while "Good Guy" and "Bounce, Shake, Move, Swing" were derivative of contemporary musical trends and

didn't play to the band's strengths. Reviews of the album were decent, with *Entertainment Weekly* calling the record, "Mature, danceable, and occasionally sexy," and the album was certified gold.

While a gold-selling record would be a dream come true for most bands, *Nathan Michael Shawn Wanya* was a commercial and critical disappointment. Following the album's release, Boyz II Men parted ways with Universal and signed a deal with Arista, which was then being run by their old collaborator, L.A. Reid. In a 2001 *Billboard* article about the label change, Nate explained, "After being released by Universal, we pretty much had our choice to go anywhere we wanted to go. [Reid] is someone who can look at what we want to do from a musical aspect as an artist and not just as a record company exec. He has been an artist before and he understands artist situations, artist mentality. So that was a major sticking point on why we went with Arista."

In the summer of 2002, Boyz II Men released their sixth studio album, *Full Circle*, a project that found the band updating their sound and experimenting with much more success than they had on the previous album. Like the best Boyz II Men projects, *Full Circle* struck a healthy balance between ballads and up-tempo jams. The band's partnership with Arista bore immediate fruit, as a formal

◄ Erykah Badu
in 2007.

relationship with L.A. Reid naturally led to a new collaboration with Babyface. This was the album's second track, "The Color of Love," which was also released as a single. While the song didn't reach the outsized sales and acclaim of their previous collaborations with Babyface, the uplifting ballad remains a favorite of Boyz II Men diehards.

While *Full Circle* is not flawless, it does reassert Boyz II Men's greatness. The vocal performances are inspiring, and the musical arrangements have some truly affecting and innovative moments. While the album was generally well received, and despite its high musicality and emotional power, *Full Circle* marked the first time a new Boyz II Men album failed to achieve even gold status in the United States.

Full Circle's lack of commercial success would not be the toughest obstacle the band had to work around during that time. Sometime in 2003, Michael either voluntarily left or was kicked out of Boyz II Men. The details of Michael's exit have been the subject of much speculation and tasteless clickbait, confusion at least partly caused by the fact that Michael and his bandmates have publicly told conflicting accounts of the separation. While all parties agree that Michael's health issues initiated the series of events that would lead to his ouster, the details conflict. Michael began experiencing severe back spasms as early

as 1993 due to multiple sclerosis, and some believe this chronic illness compromised his ability to perform live, which ultimately led him to leave the group.

In his 2016 appearance on *Iyanla, Fix My Life*, McCary spoke about his relationship with Boyz II Men, claiming that the group had abandoned him. "If I had to sum up what I got from my brothers in Boyz II Men, I would have to say betrayal, a broken bond," he said. "I mean, at this point, we don't even talk."

While Shawn has acknowledged that Michael's health was the catalyst for the split, he has also claimed that Michael didn't have a true passion for singing and would frequently miss performances the band was booked for. In a 2022 appearance on the *FAQ Podcast*, Shawn said, "Mike never really enjoyed being a singer and what I mean by that is he did it because he could. It was an opportunity, but it was never in his heart of hearts to do it like the rest of us wanted to do it. He developed scoliosis which is an irregular curvature in your spine. It affected his ability to perform. There were times where we had to work it out with Mike where while we're doing the dance steps, he's sitting on a stool. We did all types of things to try to accommodate his condition."

Shawn also said in that interview that Michael's frequent absences and lack of communication were the final straw. "But then, he started to not show up at shows," he explained. "He started to not answer our phone calls. After not answering us for weeks, he shows up at Wanyá's house. At the time, I lived around the corner from Wanyá so Wan' was like 'Yo, Mike's here, dude.' So, I'm like, 'Alright, I'll be right there.' We had planned on going to Japan in about a few weeks. *Big* payday. [Michael] heard about it . . . asked, 'Well, when are we going to Japan?' and I told him straight up, 'No . . . 'we' ain't going nowhere.'" Shawn then detailed a physical fight with Michael, after which the band kicked him out.

"We got into it. We fight. He slammed me on a table . . . on Wanyá's table. I'm trying to block punches . . . the whole nine. Mike a big guy, so I was just trying to protect my face. After I got up, I was like, 'Dude that's it. You're done'".

As difficult as Michael's exit had to have been on the group, it wasn't the only hurdle they'd have to jump in the early twenty-first century. With a looming merger between Sony Music and Arista's parent company, BMG, there were bound to be shake-ups at the executive level. Sure enough, L.A. Reid was fired as president/CEO of Arista on January 13, 2004. A little over three months later, Boyz II Men was released from their contract.

With the major labels spiraling, large indies like New York-based Koch Records were able to lure rising up-and-comers and veteran acts alike to their stable with promises of creative autonomy and a larger profit share from CD sales. In a CBS News profile on Koch, Layzie Bone of Bone Thugs-N-Harmony said, "I done got rich on Koch Records. The whole thing was very profitable. As opposed to being an artist making two dollars a record [with the major labels], we were making five dollars a record."

With an attractive royalty structure and the freedom to make the kind of music they wanted, Boyz II Men struck a partnership with Koch. The group's first Koch project, *Throwback*, was released in 2004 and consisted of covers of classic R&B songs. Adding their novel approach to vocal arrangement to beloved songs like Michael Jackson's "Human Nature," Bobby Caldwell's "What You Won't Do," Al Green's "Let's Stay Together," and more, *Throwback* reminded listeners of the band's peerless skill at interpreting other artist's songs. Over the next six years, the group closed the decade with a flurry of new albums, including their second Christmas album, 2005's *Winter/Reflections*; 2009's *The Remedy*, a fantastic album of originals; and three more covers albums: *Motown: A Journey Through Hitsville, USA* (2007), *Love* (2009), and *Covered: Winter* (2010).

On the morning of January 5, 2012, Boyz II Men received a star on the Hollywood Walk of Fame. Michael McCary rejoined the group for the dedication ceremony and Jimmy Jam, Terry Lewis, Babyface, and Michael Bivins all gave speeches. Bivins' speech was particularly moving as he spoke about working with the group at the start of their careers.

> *"Nobody really knows the journey . . . where this all really started. . . . I just remember eating turkey sandwiches in Nate's room and we was trying to figure out what we were gonna do. We were all so young and we had it on a paper plate and some paper cups . . . and from Philadelphia to Hollywood Boulevard, Mama, we did it and I'm proud of them."*

"Nobody really knows the journey . . . where this all really started. What the vision was, what the plan was and the things we had against us. To see Shawn's mom and Nate's mom . . . I just remember eating turkey sandwiches in Nate's room and we was trying to figure out what we were gonna do. We were all so young and we had it on a paper plate and some paper cups . . . and from Philadelphia to Hollywood Boulevard, Mama, we did it and I'm proud of them."

When Shawn took the stage, he gave special acknowledgments to his mother, Nathan's mother, his wife Sharonda Jones, and his son Ty (one of his twins), who was in attendance. Shawn concluded his speech with a simple admission: "This is one of the happiest days of my life." Wanyá highlighted the band's passion and love for the art form that got them to the Hollywood Walk of Fame. "If you're looking at us and could see straight through us right now," he said in his speech, "you could see that our hearts bleed music."

Although they were far from the heights of fame that they'd reached in the 1990s, Boyz II Men still holds a secure position among the most beloved and popular music groups of all time. In March 2013, Boyz II Men began a residency at the Terry Fator Theater at the Mirage Hotel and Casino in Las Vegas. Prior to Boyz II Men, not many acts from the hip-hop/R&B generation had the opportunity to get a residency on the Vegas strip. In a 2015 interview with *Las Vegas* magazine, Shawn said, "I always say Vegas is going through its second childhood. Vegas has always been known as the hot spot for the generation that is now coming, that comes to Vegas to hang out, to have fun and party. Boyz II Men represents that generation. Being there hopefully breaks down a lot of barriers. It wasn't easy for us. A lot of people didn't think that we'd work, didn't think an R&B group could have a residency in Vegas, let alone stay there for two years so far. We had a lot of obstacles, a lot of people. A lot of naysayers, nonbelievers that didn't think we could last this long. Not only is it an outward victory, but it's a personal victory for us, too. To know that so many people kind of have to eat crow because we're still here and we're putting up successful numbers."

> *"If you're looking at us and could see straight through us right now, you could see that our hearts bleed music."*

Boyz II Men took a break from the Vegas shows in the summer of 2013 to embark on the Package Tour, where they joined fellow boy bands New Kids On The Block and 98 Degrees for about fifty shows throughout the US and Canada. Then, on October 21, 2014, the band released their fourteenth studio album, *Collide*, on which the band experimented with an eclectic mixture of rock, R&B, and hip-hop.

"This time we decided to take a different approach when it comes to recording songs," Nate said of *Collide* in an interview with WBLS. "Normally we go in the studio. We create and write songs, we bring in producers. We do all this kind of stuff. This time we did a joint venture with BMG Rights, which is more of a publishing company than a record label, and they brought us a gang of songs that were incredible, and we just decided to do them. We didn't want to think about it, we didn't care who wrote it, where it came from. It didn't matter what genre it was. It didn't matter, rock record, pop record, R&B record, it didn't matter. And that's why the album is called *Collide*, because it's a bunch of songs that probably would never be on anybody else's album like this, and we decided to, you know, make them collide all together on this record."

"We wanted to take music away from the genre-driven, you know, style," Wanyá added. "People know Boyz II Men as R&B singers, but we wanted them to actually open up their minds and set aside the preconceived notion of Boyz II Men, to recognize the music, the lyrical content, the feeling, the vibe."

As three of the best singers and vocal arrangers of their generation, Shawn, Nathan, and Wanyá's talents make the songs on *Collide* work—for the most part. Songs like "Diamond Eyes," "Believe Us," and the folksy jam "As Long As I'm With You" are a little corny but provide welcome twists in the band's slow

▼ Boyz II Men perform at the Total Package Tour's stop in Las Vegas at the Mandalay Bay Events Center, 2013.

jam-heavy catalog. The critical reception to *Collide* was tepid at best. The *Guardian*'s Tshepo Mokoena called the album's open approach to genre "confusing" and "unfocused" in a 2014 review. That summer, Nate, Shawn, and Wanyá sat down for an in-depth interview about their career with Larry King on Ora TV, an on-demand digital television network that was launched in 2012 by King and his wife Shawn Southwick King. It was a wide-ranging and insightful conversation, covering everything from technology and the music business to Michael's exit from the group and Boyz II Men's longevity. Nate leaves viewers with a poignant reminder of what keeps Boyz II Men together after all these years: "We know who we are first and we've been with each other forever. We fight like brothers and family. No matter what it is, it's all about the friendship."

> *"People know Boyz II Men as R&B singers, but we wanted them to actually open up their minds and set aside the preconceived notion of Boyz II Men, to recognize the music, the lyrical content, the feeling, the vibe."*

U KNOW

"In February 2023, I got an invite to a private Boyz II Men show at the anniversary of the Hard Rock Café on Market Street in Philadelphia. This was my moment. As soon as I arrived, I planted myself firmly at the front of the waist-level stage, ready to wait however long it took to see the performance of a lifetime. As they made their way to the back of the stage to grab their roses [during 'I'll Make Love To You'], I couldn't help but smile and be grateful to be there and listen to some of the most talented voices alive. In a moment, less than a foot away, Nathan's hand outstretched to deliver me not just a rose, but the first one of the entire song." —*Scarlet Estelle-Hernandez, fan*

A BEHIND-THE-SCENES
INTERVIEW WITH . . .

DARIA MARMALUK-HAJIOANNOU IS A WORLD AND CHILDREN'S MUSICIAN. AS A SKILLED MULTI-INSTRUMENTALIST, A KEY COMPONENT OF HAJIOANNOU'S WORK IS EDUCATING YOUNG PEOPLE AND ADULTS ABOUT MUSIC CULTURES FROM AROUND THE WORLD. IN THE 1990S, HAJIOANNOU WORKED AS THE STUDIO MANAGER AT BOYZ II MEN'S STONECREEK STUDIO ALONGSIDE HER HUSBAND, GEORGE HAJIOANNOU.

▶ **CAN YOU TALK A LITTLE BIT ABOUT YOUR BACKGROUND IN MUSIC?**

I was raised in the United States and also in Peru, and through all my permutations I became a world music artist. But, you know, when you're in your twenties, thirties, there really isn't a paying spot for that kind of work. When George and I met, we fell in love and, you know, the opportunity came up to run the studio.

▶ **DID YOU MEET BOYZ II MEN THROUGH GEORGE? HOW DID YOU GET THE JOB AS STUDIO MANAGER AT STONECREEK?**

Boyz II Men were George's clients, and I think that Nate had really come to trust George. I won't say we hung out, but we knew each other. One time, I drove Nate to IKEA and kept him safe from all the fans. [laughs] So, it was one of those things where they kind of knew us as friends. So, it was just kind of natural for me to work with them through the construction period and into the opening.

▶ **AND YOU HAD PRIOR EXPERIENCE MANAGING AND WORKING IN RECORDING STUDIOS?**

Yeah, I'd worked at a few studios and I took an audio engineering course because everybody talked down to women and I figured if I took the engineering course I could tell people, "Your microphone's out of phase" and know what I was talking about, rather than, "You're just a dumb girl, you don't know what you're saying . . ." It really helped to know what was in the studio, how it worked, and how to fix it when something went wrong.

▶ **WHAT WAS YOUR DAY-TO-DAY WORK LIKE AS A MANAGER AT STONECREEK?**

It really was so different from day to day. Once the studio was up and running, we would just make sure all the staff knew that the boys were coming in, who was coming in, letting the engineer know he'd be there, if they needed studio musicians. It was just totally different

every time. Shawn would just sometimes come in to compose in his room and he'd say, "I'm hungry, can you order me this?" So it was really just being a buffer, making sure that when they needed something to be comfortable they had it, which were usually things like cheesesteaks. When other celebrities came in, you kind of ran interference because there would always be the person trying to sneak in or get an autograph or get a picture, or they just want to meet Wanyá. A lot of it was keeping your bosses from having to be interrupted when they were working.

▶ **HOW LONG WERE YOU AT STONECREEK?**

I think it was about a year, maybe a little bit more. I had a newborn and it was kind of hard juggling childcare. So when they started to kind of ramp down and consider selling and whatever, it just was the right time to say, "We're just gonna do less." I had a secretary and she took over and it was kind of worked out.

▶ **WHAT ARE SOME SIGNIFICANT MEMORIES THAT STOOD OUT ABOUT YOUR TIME WITH BOYZ II MEN AT STONECREEK?**

It was just joy and fun, you know? One time, I was there with my daughter and [actor] Alfonso Ribeiro sang her the most beautiful version of "Happy Birthday." [Boyz II Men] attracted good people and that says something about the quality of their art and the quality of who they were.

CONCLUSION

NEARLY THIRTY-FIVE YEARS after the release of *Cooleyhighharmony*, Boyz II Men have solidified their status as a legacy act and one of the defining groups of the 1990s. Once they went independent, with their days on the top of the pop charts behind them, the group spent the 2010s working their small corner of the music business on their own terms. In a 2021 interview with Philadelphia Magazine, Nate explained to writer Patrick Rapa that the group was comfortable with their current status.

"That's our creative freedom. That gives us the ability to do whatever we want to do," he said, reflecting on making the music that they want to make without the obstructions and headaches that come with working for a major label. "Because for the last fifteen, sixteen, maybe twenty years now, we haven't really had to depend on a record label for anything. The pressure of having to come up with a new hit and people telling you how you've got to make the record, I guess I'm too old for that."

While the group was no longer battling it out on the charts with the popular artists of the day, they were in no way inactive. On November 19, 2014, Boyz II Men performed for Billy Joel when he was awarded the Library of Congress Prize for Popular Song. Created in 2007, the annual award is given to composers who have made significant contributions to popular music. Prior honorees include Paul Simon (who received the inaugural award), Joni Mitchell, Paul McCartney, Smokey Robinson, and Stevie Wonder.

The 2014 ceremony for Joel was hosted at the DAR Constitution Hall in Washington, DC, and included a star-studded lineup of guests. Along with Boyz II Men, the evening's lineup featured Tony Bennett, Gavin DeGraw, Josh Groban, Natalie Maines, John Mellencamp, and LeAnn Rimes, with each act performing a song from Joel's vast catalog. Boyz II Men chose Joel's "The Longest Time," from the 1983 album *An Innocent Man*. "The Longest Time"

▼ Boyz II Men in front of the Mirage Hotel in Las Vegas to announce their extended residency in 2013.

originated from a demo that Joel recorded in 1981 called *Prime of Your Life*. Wanting to pay homage to the doo-wop and early rock 'n' roll of the 1950s and 1960s that influenced him, Joel stripped away the piano part from *Prime of Your Life* and altered the lyrics to rework it into a doo-wop homage. In Boyz II Men's hands, "The Longest Time" is a revelation, given new life by Shawn, Nate, and Wanyá.

As the Vegas residency was still going strong—the group won Casino Entertainment Awards' Musical Artist of the Year in October 2014—Boyz II Men got calls for other performance opportunities off the Strip. In December 2014, the group made their way to Europe for dates in London, Birmingham, and Manchester in the UK, and in Brussels, Belgium. On January 16, 2015, the group opened the new year by celebrating the second anniversary of their residency at the Terry Fator Theatre. In a 2017 interview with Yahoo's Build Series, Nate said of the Vegas residencies, "We kinda didn't really know what to expect when we first got there. The only thing we did know is that it would stop us from running around the world every other week 'cause before we did Vegas, we'd be in Asia one week and we'd be here for two weeks and then we'd go somewhere for a month. We're now realizing that all our fans from around the world can come to one central location and see our show."

Vegas provided the band with both a steady gig and the flexibility to pursue interesting one-off performances. In March 2015, Boyz II Men went to Nashville for a three-night engagement at the Schermerhorn Symphony Center, as part of the FirstBank Pops Series in which the Nashville Symphony backed eight leading acts, including the Four Tops, Kenny Rogers, Styx, and Kenny G. The performances provided Boyz II Men with an opportunity to revisit some of the classical training they'd received at CAPA.

"We come from a high school where we sang classical," Shawn said in a pre-show interview with Nashville's *Tennessean*. "We sang Tchaikovsky and Bach and Brahms and Mozart and all of those other great composers. We used to read music and all of that other stuff. So we were very versed when it came to the type of music we sang, it wasn't just R&B music. We learned about mezzo forte and pizzicato. I haven't read music in a while, so I'm kind of rusty, but I guess after a couple of days, it's like riding a bike. This is something that we've always done. It's almost like a homecoming to some degree."

Fresh off the Nashville performances, the group returned to Europe in May 2015 for their first UK tour with a full band. In an April 2015 interview with the *Glasgow Times* ahead of a May 5 show at Glasgow's O2 Academy, Shawn said, "We love Scotland. It's

◄ Boyz II Men perform at the 2015 Soul Train Music Awards in Las Vegas.

beautiful—like something out of a storybook. The Scottish people show so much love—and they're great fun. They're just really in touch with hip-hop and R&B, as much as people across the pond in the States. We're so looking forward to coming back."

Following stops in Newcastle, Hull, Manchester, Bristol, Birmingham, and London, in a Gigwise.com review of the May 13 show at the O2 in London, writer Drew Heatley gushed over the group's performance. "'It's So Hard To Say Goodbye To Yesterday' is a showstopper. Delivered completely a cappella, it's easy to see why almost every vocal group of the last two decades list Boyz II Men as an inspiration," Heatley wrote. "The refreshing thing about this show is how much fun the group is having. Shawn constantly has a smile on his face, there's larking around (including onstage selfies with a fan's smartphone) and plenty of dance routines. Even after this long, Boyz II Men aren't just going through the motions."

Eight days after the UK tour's closing night in London, Boyz II Men were back at the Mirage in Las Vegas, where they would remain for the bulk of the summer of 2015. In October, they toured New Zealand and Australia, then made an appearance at the 2015 Soul Train Music Awards to pay tribute to Babyface, who was presented with the Soul Train Legend Award. As part of the celebration of Babyface's career, Boyz II Men sang "I'll Make Love To You" and "End Of The Road" with the same emotional weight and passion that they've brought to those songs countless times before.

With the group commuting to Vegas to perform every weekend throughout 2016, they still had to find time to record a new album. "We're very busy, we have shows every week, the residency in Vegas and we have families and stuff like that, too, so it's almost like you have to get it in where you can fit it in," Wanyá explained in a 2018 interview with the Sirius XM radio show, *The Happy Hour with Heather B.* Recorded in studios across Florida and Los Angeles and released in October 2017, the group's next album, *Under the Streetlight*, returned them to doo-wop and old-school rhythm and blues sounds. The album is mostly covers of 1950s and early 1960s songs, including inspired reinterpretations of Little Anthony and the Imperials' "Tears On My Pillow," The Flamingos' "I Only Have Eyes For You," Etta James' "A Sunday Kind Of Love," and more. Topped off with guest appearances

▲ WanMor members Tyvas, Rocco, Chulo,
and Big Boy—all Wayná's sons—performing
at the 65th Grammy Awards in 2023.

from Brian McKnight, Amber Riley, Take 6, and Jimmy Merchant, *Under the Streetlight* is a loving presentation of some of the most beloved American popular songs.

Despite the songs' familiarity, Boyz II Men freshen up these classics with vocal performances that blend the old with the new. Andy Kellerman's Allmusic.com review positions *Under the Streetlight* as an artistically successful—if safe—departure from the experimental eclecticism of *Collide*, saying the group "could probably knock out similar projects every few weeks and consistently attract listeners who won't tire of hearing refreshed classics."

As of this writing, *Under the Streetlight* is Boyz II Men's last album, though Nate, Shawn, and Wanyá still regularly tour the US and overseas. In August 2018, Bruno Mars announced that the group would be joining him on the closing North American leg of his massive 24K Magic Tour. The group's pioneering fusion of doo-wop, hip-hop, and contemporary R&B was a clear influence on the retro-styled sound that Mars had carved out on albums like 2010's *Doo-Wops & Hooligans* and 2016's *XXIVK Magic*. In a 2016 interview with the renowned British music publication *NME*, Mars explained,

"That was my childhood; that's why I fell in love with music. Those '90s songs are what I was singing to get the girls in school, the songs that the girls like, what we were dancing to as children. New Edition. Boyz II Men. Blackstreet. Mint Condition. Babyface. Jimmy Jam. Terry Lewis. Teddy Riley. I think that the reason why that music resonates so much for me is that it made it okay to dance—it was cool to dance. It was cool to be joyous, to have fun and wear some flashy shit. It was cool to fall in love and smile and flirt on the dance floor."

Boyz II Men joined the 24K Magic Tour in early September 2018. Susan, a fan who attended the show at Denver's Pepsi Center, called it "mesmerizing" and praised both Boyz II Men and Bruno Mars' performances: "Legendary Boyz II Men began the evening and instantly brought the audience and myself back to the day."

The tour stopped in Philly on September 19. By all accounts, the evening was a successful homecoming, and the band was welcomed accordingly by the hometown crowd. In a review for the *Philadelphia Daily News*, Drew Lazor recalled that the band played a tight set to an enthusiastic response: "The Philadelphia natives earned a predictably exuberant ovation from the Wells Fargo Center, conducting a taut hit train that began with 'Motownphilly' and made all the scheduled stops ('On Bended Knee,' 'End Of The Road,' 'Water Runs Dry')."

After the Bruno Mars tour, Boyz II Men returned to their Vegas residency at the Mirage. After six years there (from 2013–2019), the band embarked on a new residency in 2024 at the Chelsea at the Cosmopolitan in Las Vegas. In addition to this steady touring and residency work, the last few years have been kind to Boyz II Men and their legacy. In the social media age, the group has seen a resurgence of sorts with WanMor, the singing group made up of Wanyá's sons: Wanyá Morris II aka "Big Boy," Wanyá III aka "Chulo," Wanyá IV aka "Tyvas," and Wanyá V aka "Rocco." WanMor's viral videos have been making noise on Instagram, and popular Boyz II Men-related trends like the End Of The Road Harmony Challenge have popped off on TikTok in recent years.

Yet a vital part of the Boyz II Men story has remained largely unresolved. When we met Boyz II Men way back in 1991, they were a unit, a brotherhood of gifted young men. Michael's exit has not sat well with many fans.

On Friday, August 30, 2024, the group made a key step toward healing the fracture. As they performed on stage at the Chelsea, Michael joined Nate, Shawn, and Wanyá for the first time since 2003. While there have been no reunion announcements as of the writing of this book, the news of Michael's appearance and the subsequent Instagram post showing the four men smiling together backstage swept through the music world like a wave of joy and relief. The quartet of gifted young men that we'd all rooted for and admired throughout the 1990s were back together again, if only for one night.

Today, Boyz II Men occupies a distinct place in popular culture. The band's greatest hits are still a vital part of weddings, dance parties, and family reunions around the world. Vocal groups may have fallen out of favor, but the contributions that Boyz II Men made to the art of singing—that most intimate and human of musical performance—cannot be underestimated. The emotional depth and musical complexities that Nathan Morris, Shawn Stockman, Wanyá Morris, and Michael McCary wrung out of the human voice have profoundly enriched our understanding of what music can be.

▶ The group performs at the Stay In School Rally in 1995.

TIMELINE

—

1985
Nathan Morris and Marc Nelson form the group Unique Attraction at the Philadelphia School for the Creative and Performing Arts.

1988
Following lineup changes, Unique Attraction becomes Boyz II Men.

May 10, 1989: Boyz II Men sneak back-stage at a concert in Philly and audition for Michael Bivins. Bivins later agrees to man-age the group and they sign to Motown.

1991
April 30, 1991: Boyz II Men releases their debut album, *Cooleyhighharmony*.

1992
The band heads out on their first major tour opening for MC Hammer.

May 25, 1992: Boyz II Men's road manager, Roderick "Khalil" Rountree, is tragically murdered in Chicago.

June 30, 1992: "End Of The Road" is released.

August 15, 1992: "End Of The Road" reaches No. 1 on the *Billboard* Hot 100 chart. The song goes on to spend thirteen consecutive weeks at No. 1, breaking Elvis Presley's record for "Don't Be Cruel/Hound Dog" from 1956.

1993
January 19, 1993: Boyz II Men perform for the Presidential Inaugural Celebration for Youth.

February 24, 1993: "End Of The Road" wins the Grammy for Best R&B Performance by a Duo or Group with Vocal. "End Of The Road" also wins the Best Rhythm & Blues Song award for Babyface, L.A. Reid, and Daryl Simmons.

1994
July 26, 1994: Boyz II Men releases "I'll Make Love To You."

August 27, 1994: "I'll Make Love To You" hits No. 1 on the *Billboard* Hot 100. The song will remain at No. 1 for fourteen consecutive weeks, breaking the record set by "End Of The Road."

August 30, 1994: Boyz II Men releases the album *II*.

November 1, 1994: Boyz II Men releases "On Bended Knee."

▲ Boyz II Men and Michael Bivins
(center) attend the 34th Annual
Grammy Awards in 1992.

1995

January 1, 1995: Boyz II Men start the All Around The World Tour.

March 1995: Boyz II Men finalize the lease of a new studio in Gladwyne, Pennsylvania. The group christen the space Stonecreek Studio.

June 22, 1995: Boyz II Men pay tribute to Michael Jackson during the VH1 Honors.

November 7, 1995: Boyz II Men release *The Remix Collection*.

November 14, 1995: Mariah Carey and Boyz II Men release "One Sweet Day."

October 1995: LL Cool J releases "Hey Lover," featuring Boyz II Men.

1996

February 28, 1996: Boyz II Men are nominated for two Grammys, Record of the Year (for "One Sweet Day") and Best Pop Collaboration with Vocals (also for "One Sweet Day").

1997

September 23, 1997: Boyz II Men release *Evolution*.

1998

July 28, 1998: Boyz II Men release "Doin' Just Fine."

2000

August 28, 2000: The group releases "Pass You By."

September 12, 2000: Boyz II Men release *Nathan Michael Shawn Wanya*.

November 20, 2000: Boyz II Men perform at Soul Train Christmas Starfest 2000.

December 12, 2000: Boyz II Men release "Thank You In Advance."

▶ Celebrating Boyz II Men at their Walk of Fame ceremony in 2012.

2002
June 11, 2002: Boyz II Men release "The Color of Love."

June 11, 2002: Boyz II Men release *Full Circle*.

2003
Michael McCary leaves Boyz II Men.

2004
August 24, 2004: Boyz II Men release *Throwback, Vol. 1*.

2007
November 13, 2007: Boyz II Men release *Motown: A Journey Through Hitsville, USA*.

2012
January 5, 2012: Boyz II Men receive a star on the Hollywood Walk of Fame.

2013
March 2013: Boyz II Men begin a residency at the Mirage in Las Vegas.

2018
September 2018: Boyz II Men join Bruno Mars' 24K Magic Tour.

2024
Boyz II Men begin a new residency at the Chelsea at the Cosmopolitan in Las Vegas.

August 30, 2024: Michael McCary makes an appearance onstage with the group at the Chelsea.

DISCOGRAPHY

ALBUMS

Cooleyhighharmony

Original Release: April 30, 1991
Record Label: Motown
Sales: 9,000,000 US (9.4 million world-wide)

Singles:
"Motownphilly"
(April 30, 1991)

"It's So Hard To Say Goodbye To Yesterday"
(August 20, 1991)

"Uhh Ahh"
(November 26, 1991)

"Please Don't Go"
(March 17, 1992)

"End Of The Road"
(June 30, 1992)

"In The Still Of The Nite (I'll Remember)"
(November 10, 1992)

Christmas Interpretations

Original Release: October 5, 1993
Record Label: Motown
Sales: 2,000,000 US (2 million worldwide)

II

Original Release: August 30, 1994
Record Label: Motown
Sales: 12,000,000 US (13.9 million worldwide)

Singles:
"I'll Make Love To You"
(July 26, 1994)

"On Bended Knee"
(November 1, 1994)

"Thank You"
(February 7, 1995)

"Water Runs Dry"
(April 11, 1995)

Evolution

Original Release: September 23, 1997
Record Label: Motown
Sales: 2,000,000 US (2.7 million worldwide)

Singles:
"4 Seasons of Loneliness"
(September 8, 1997)

"A Song For Mama"
(November 25, 1997)

"Can't Let Her Go"
(March 20, 1998)

"Doin' Just Fine"
(July 28, 1998)

Nathan Michael Shawn Wanya

Original Release: September 12, 2000
Record Label: Universal
Sales: 800,000 US (800,000 worldwide)

Singles:
"Pass You By"
(August 28, 2000)

"Thank You In Advance"
(December 12, 2000)

Full Circle

Original Release: June 11, 2002
Record Label: Arista
Sales: 243,000 US (243,000 worldwide)

Singles:
"The Color of Love"
(June 11, 2002)

"Relax Your Mind"
(July 16, 2002)

Throwback, Vol. 1

Original Release: August 24, 2004
Record Label: Koch, MSM
Sales: 38,148 in Japan

Singles:
"What You Won't Do"
(August 24, 2004)

"You Make Me Feel"
(2004)

"I Miss You"
(2004)

"Sarah Smile"
(2005)

The Remedy

Original Release: October 25,
2006
Record Label: Koch, MSM

Motown: A Journey Through Hitsville, USA

Original Release: November 13,
2007
Label: Decca

Singles:
"Just My Imagination (Running
Away With Me)"
(2007)

"It's The Same Old Song/Reach
Out I'll Be There"
(2007)

"Ribbon In The Sky"
(2007)

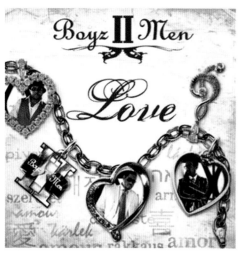  

Love

Original Release: November 24, 2009
Record Label: Decca

Covered: Winter

Original Release: December 22, 2010
Record Label: MSM, Rhythm Zone

Twenty

Original Release: October 25, 2011
Record Label: MSM, Benchmark

Singles:
"More Than You'll Ever Know"
(feat. Charlie Wilson)
(November 9, 2011)

"One More Dance"
(2012)

 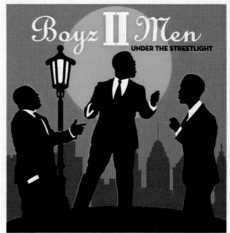

Collide

Original Release: October 21, 2014
Record Label: BMG, MSM

Under the Streetlight

Original Release: October 20, 2017
Label: Tango, MasterWorks, MSM

Singles

"Comin' Home Baby"
Michael Bublé Duet With Boyz II Men
Original Release: 2007
Warner Music/Benelux

"One Up For Love / Flow"
Original Release: October 24, 2011
Universal Music Group International

"You Just Got Slapped" (from *How I Met Your Mother*)
Original Release: January 1, 2012
20th Century Fox Records

"Better Half"
Original Release: 2014

"Love Struck" (from *Songland*)
Original Release: June 25, 2019
MSM Music Group

"House Party" (New Kids On The Block, Boyz II Men, Big Freedia, Naughty By Nature, Jordin Sparks)
Original Release: April 24, 2020
NKOTB Music

ACKNOWLEDGMENTS

I want to start by expressing deep respect, and appreciation to my partner and the love of my life, Melissa Simpson. I couldn't imagine completing this book without your support, counsel, and love. Much love to my mom and best friend, Jackqueline Morrison. You are the reason why I have dedicated my life to art, creativity, and imagination. Thank you and I love you.

Shout out to my brother, Devin Roache, Relonda, and Shamir Roache. My sisters, Kelly Morrison Smith and Schenda Morrison. Josh Leidy, Steve Clark, Notus Williams, Justin Zugerman, Ayahna Kadir, DuiJi Mshinda, Shawanda Spivey, all my aunties, uncs, cousins, and fam in Philly and around the world.

Thanks and deep appreciation to everyone who's taken the time to read my work. Thank you to all the talented journalists and musicians that spoke to me for this book. I literally couldn't have done it without y'all. Extra special thank you to my editor, Katie McGuire, for all your help, insight, and patience. Thank you to Cara Donaldson and the entire team at Epic Ink/Quarto.

Much respect and thank you to Shawn Stockman, Wanyá Morris, Nate Morris, and Michael McCary for gifting us with years of brilliant, soul-stirring music. It's been a pleasure to write about your work.

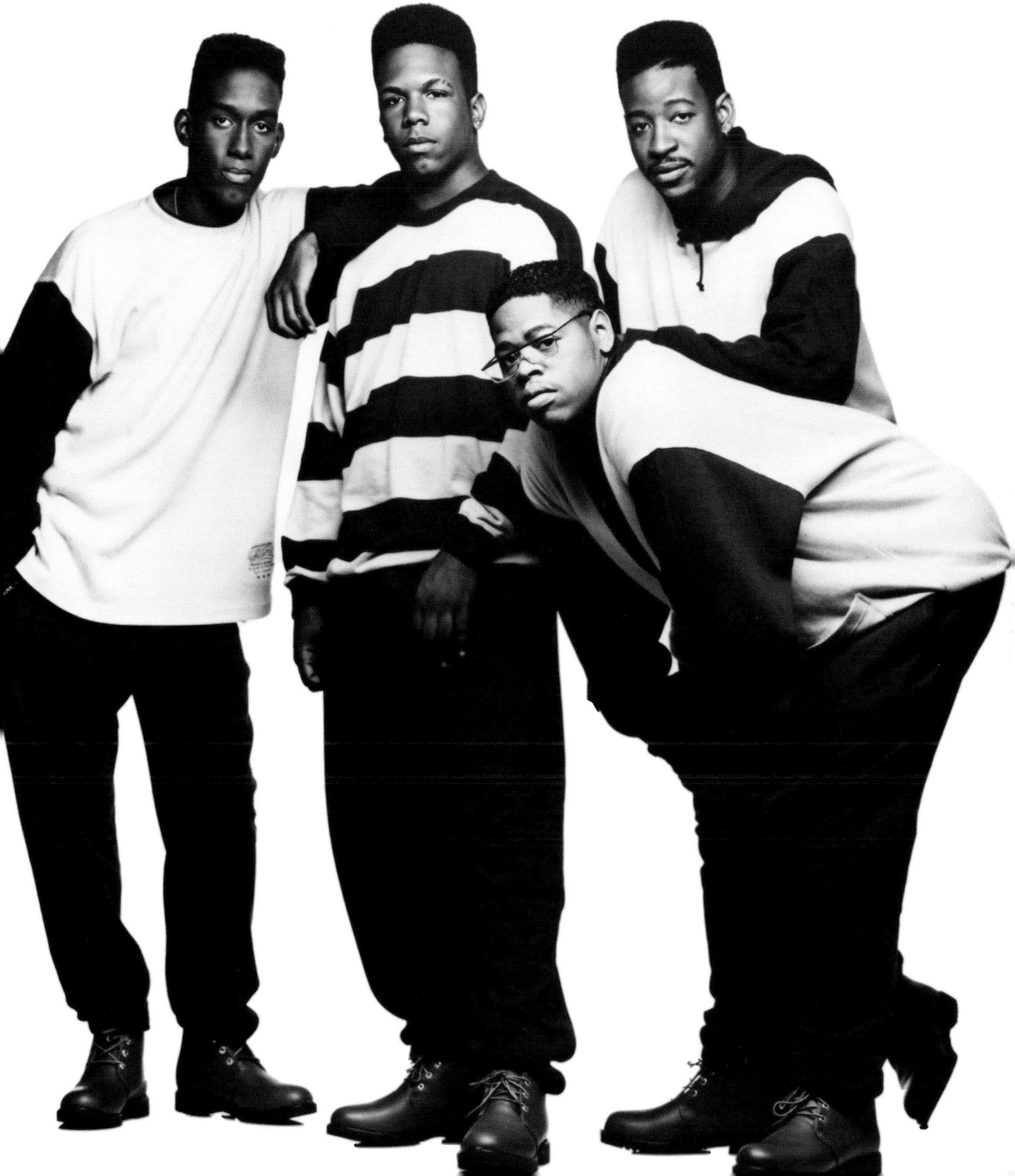

▼ Boyz II Men photographed in the 1990s.

ABOUT THE AUTHOR

John Morrison is a writer, producer, and DJ from Philadelphia. For the last twenty-five years, Morrison has worked as an independent music journalist, documenting and reporting on Philly hip-hop culture. His writing has appeared in the *Philadelphia City Paper*, *NPR Music*, *The Wire*, Red Bull Music Academy, Bandcamp Daily, and more. An in-demand on-air personality, Morrison regularly appears on NPR's *All Songs Considered* and *The World Cafe*, as well as NPR's Tiny Desk Top Shelf series.

Morrison is currently writing a major book on the history of hip-hop culture in Philadelphia. Exploring hip-hop's first major stronghold outside New York, Morrison's book will fill in some crucial blank spaces about the dawn of hip-hop and its eventual nationwide spread.

▲ The band rehearses for the
Billboard Music Awards in 1992.

IMAGE CREDITS

PAGE 2 Afro Newspaper/Gado/Archive Photos/Getty Images. PAGE 4-5 Afro Newspaper/Gado/Archive Photos/ Getty Images. PAGE 9 Vinnie Zuffante/Stringer/Archive Photos/Getty Images. PAGE 10-11 Raymond Boyd/ Michael Ochs Archives/Getty images. PAGE 12-13 Raymond Boyd/Michael Ochs Archives/Getty Images. PAGE 14 Gilles Petard/Redferns/Getty Images. PAGE 17 LEFT AND ABOVE RIGHT: Everett Collection, Inc./ Alamy Stock Photo. BELOW RIGHT: Allstar Picture Library Ltd/Alamy Stock Photo. PAGE 18 Michael Ochs Archives/Stringer/Getty Images. PAGE 21 Michael Ochs Archives/Stringer/Getty Images. PAGE 22 Vinnie Zuffante/Stringer/Archive Photos/Getty Images. PAGE 25 Jeff Kravitz/FilmMagic, Inc/Getty Images. PAGE 26-27 Eric Fougere/Sygma/Getty Images. PAGE 30-31 Afro Newspaper/Gado/Archive Photos/Getty Images. PAGE 32 Bastiaan Slabbers/OOgImages / Alamy Stock Photo. PAGE 35 Gilbert Carrasquillo/GC Images/Getty Images. PAGE 36 Taylor Hill/Getty Images Entertainment. PAGE 39 Afro Newspaper/Gado/Archive Photos/Getty Images. PAGE 40-41 Bettmann/Getty Images. PAGE 42 Gems/RedfernsGetty Images. PAGE 44-45 Pictorial Press Ltd/Alamy Stock Photo. PAGE 46 Michael Ochs Archives/Stringer/Getty Images. PAGE 49 Gie Knaeps/Hulton Archive/Getty Images. PAGE 52 Michael Ochs Archives/Stringer/Getty Images. PAGE 54 Records/Alamy Stock Photo. PAGE 59 Al Pereira/Michael Ochs Archives/Getty Images. PAGE 60-61 Afro Newspaper/Gado/Archive Photos/Getty Images. PAGE 65 WENN Rights Ltd/Alamy Stock Photo. PAGE 66-67 MediaPunch Inc/Alamy Stock Photo. PAGE 69 Vinnie Zuffante/Stringer/Archive Photos/Getty Images. PAGE 70 Everett Collection, Inc. PAGE 73 Vinnie Zuffante/Stringer. PAGE 74 Al Pereira/Michael Ochs Archives/Getty Images. PAGE 77 Soul Train/Getty Images. PAGE 81 Afro Newspaper/Gado/Archive Photos/Getty Images. PAGE 82-83 dpa picture alliance/Alamy Stock Photo. PAGE 85 Houston Chronicle/Hearst Newspapers/Hearst Newspapers/Getty Images. PAGE 86 BSR Entertainment/Getty Images. PAGE 88-89 Denise Sofranko/Michael Ochs Archives/ Getty Images. PAGE 91 Harry Langdon/Archive Photos/Getty Images. PAGE 95 Raymond Boyd/Michael Ochs Archives/Getty images. PAGE 96-97 Vinnie Zuffante/Stringer/Archive Photos/Getty Images. PAGE 98 Phil Dent/Redferns/Getty Images. PAGE 101 Lynn Goldsmith/Corbis Historical. PAGE 102 Vinnie Zuffante/Stringer/Archive Photos/Getty Images.

SOURCES

Boyz II Men. *Us II You*. New York, NY: HarperCollins, 1995

Canfield, Jack, Mark Victor Hansen, and Jo-Ann Geffen. *Chicken Soup for the Soul: The Story Behind the Song*. New York, NY: Simon & Schuster, 2009.

Considine, J.D. "The Remix Collection." Baltimore Sun, 7 Dec. 1995. https://www.newspapers.com/image/171347186/

DeLuca, Dan. "Boyz II Men deadline a wholesome R&B bill." Philadelphia Inquirer, 17 Jan. 1995. https://philly.newspapers.com/image/178019264/.

George, Nelson. *The Death of Rhythm & Blues*. New York, NY: Pantheon, 1988.

Griffin, Gil. "Hip Hop, Rap Fans Find Stations Are Tuning Them Out." Washington Post, 21 Mar. 1991. www.washingtonpost.com/archive/local/1991/03/21/sounds/b131a3d0-d692-4dbd-8493-27357819b11d/.

Kellman, Andy. "Under The Streetlight." Allmusic.com, 20 Oct. 2017. https://www.allmusic.com/album/under-the-streetlight-mw0003101977.

Mokena, Tshepo. "Boyz II Men: Collide review – enough genre-hopping to give you whiplash." The Guardian, 4 Dec. 2014. https://www.theguardian.com/music/2014/dec/04/boyz-ii-men-collide-review.

Murray, Laura. "Student Gets Ball Rolling Against Gym Thefts." Philadelphia Daily News, 20 Dec. 1977. https://philly.newspapers.com/image/185372490/.

Murray, Laura. "Arts School Deadline Near." Philadelphia Daily News, 9 Jan. 1978. https://philly.newspapers.com/image/185280544/.

Phalen, Tom. "Boyz II Men Concert: It Starts Young but Matures Quickly." Seattle Times, 21 Mar. 1995. https://archive.seattletimes.com/archive/19950321/2111382/boyz-ii-men-concert-it-starts-young-but-matures-quickly.

Rapa, Patrick. "Why, 30 Years Later, the World Still Loves Boyz II Men." Philadelphia Magazine, 28 Aug. 2021. https://www.phillymag.com/news/2021/08/28/boyz-ii-men/.

Staff Report. "Boyz II Men Evolve from Warmup Group to Headlining Act." The Morning Call, 31 Aug. 1995. https://www.mcall.com/1995/08/31/boyz-ii-men-evolve-from-warm-up-group-to-headlining-act/.

Takiff, Jonathan. "A Broadway Wannabe?" Philadelphia Daily News, 23 Apr. 1992, https://philly.newspapers.com/image/184551613/.

Thompson, Ahmir "Questlove." *Mo' Meta Blues: The World According to Questlove*. New York, NY: Grand Central Publishing, 2013.

Ware, Lawrence. "Boyz II Men's Christmas Interpretations is One of the Best Christmas Albums of the Last 50 Years." Counterpunch, 2 Dec. 2022. https://www.counterpunch.org/2022/12/02/boyz-ii-mens-christmas-interpretations-is-one-of-the-best-christmas-albums-of-the-last-50-years/.

INDEX

► Boyz II Men perform the National Anthem at Levi's Stadium in Santa Clara, California, in September 2024.

First published in 2025 by Epic Ink, an imprint of The Quarto Group,
142 West 36th Street, 4th Floor, New York, NY 10018, USA
(212) 779-4972 • www.Quarto.com

Epic Ink titles are also available at discount for retail, wholesale, promotional, and bulk purchase.
For details, contact the Special Sales Manager by email at specialsales@quarto.com or by mail at The
Quarto Group, Attn: Special Sales Manager, 100 Cummings Center Suite 265D, Beverly, MA 01915 USA.

10 9 8 7 6 5 4 3 2 1

ISBN: 978-0-7603-9502-8

Digital edition published in 2025
eISBN: 978-0-7603-9503-5

Library of Congress Control Number: 2024950051

Group Publisher: Rage Kindelsperger
Creative Director: Laura Drew
Managing Editor: Cara Donaldson
Editor: Katie McGuire
Cover and Interior Design: Raphael Geroni

Printed in China

BOYZ MEN BOYZ MEN

MEN BOYZ MEN BOYZ

BOYZ MEN BOYZ MEN

MEN BOYZ MEN BOYZ

BOYZ MEN BOYZ MEN

MEN BOYZ MEN BOYZ

BOYZ MEN BOYZ MEN

40TH ANNIVERSARY CELEBRATION ▲

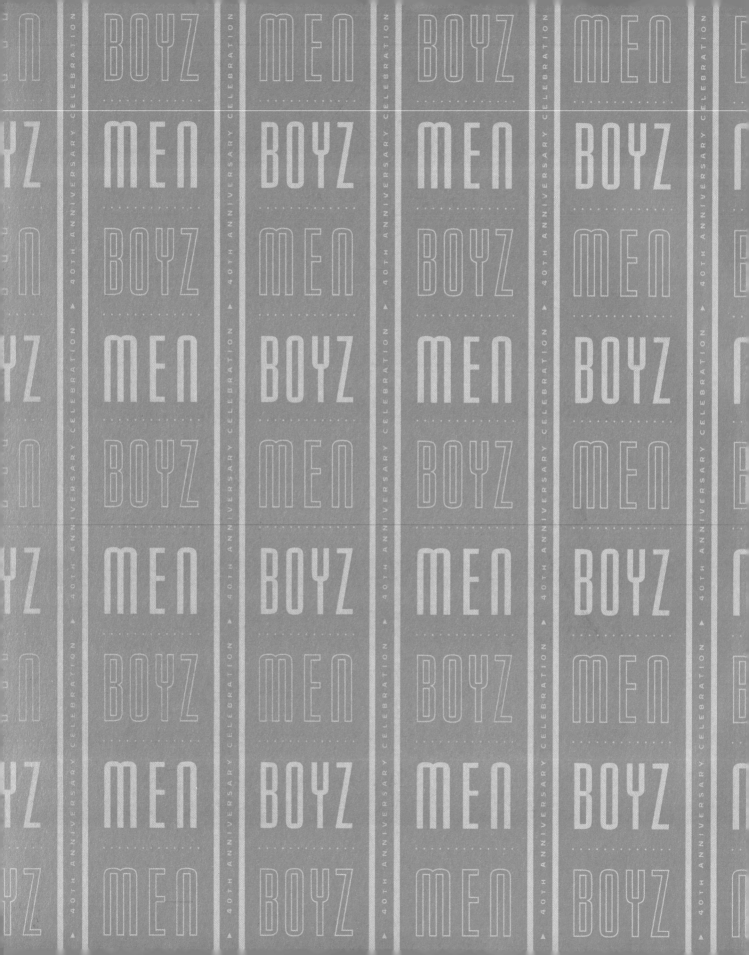